THE AWAKENING...

Eternal Youth, Vibrant Health, Radiant Beauty

Patricia Diane Cota-Robles

The New Age Study of Humanity's Purpose, Inc.
P.O. Box 41883
Tucson, Arizona 85717
U.S.A.
Telephone: 602/885-7909
Fax: 602/323-8252

New Age Study of Humanity's Purpose, Inc.
P.O. Box 41883
Tucson, AZ 85717

Cover and Illustrations by Sharon Maia Nichols
For information on Visionary Art by Sharon Maia Nichols, contact
The New Age Study of Humanity's Purpose
PO Box 41883
Tucson, AZ 85717

Manufactured in the United States of America

Library of Congress Cataloging in Publication Date
ISBN 0-9615287-3-7

First Edition January 11, 1993

DEDICATION

This book is lovingly dedicated to the **Holy Christ Self** blazing in every human Heart--the Divine Presence of every man, woman and child, Who is at long last bursting the bonds of human limitation and taking full dominion of our physical, etheric, mental and emotional bodies.

INTRODUCTION

Hi Beautiful Sons and Daughters of God,

Isn't it exciting to hear those words and know that at long last we are finally in a position to actually outpicture the radiant physical bodies that truly warrant being called Sons and Daughters of God? We have been suffering on what has been known as the "wheel of karma" for literally millions of years. This was the path of darkness that Humanity fell to when we began to use our creative faculties of thought and feeling in ways that were conflicting with God's Will.

The "wheel of karma" was the path of separation, the path of the duality of good and evil, the path of lack and limitation. It was the path of pain and suffering, the path of poverty, disease, aging, death and all manner of human miscreation.

The "wheel of karma" was a gross distortion of the Divine Plan on Earth. It was a mutation of the Law of the Circle, and it has oppressed Humanity and held us prisoners in an endless cycle of rebirth, suffering and death. But, now, at long last, IT'S OVER!!!

Through the mercy of our Father-Mother God and the unified efforts of millions of Lightworkers throughout the world, we have moved from the seemingly endless "wheel of karma," and we have ascended back onto the *Spiral of Evolution,* which was our original Divine Path prior to the fall of Humanity. It is difficult for us to truly grasp the magnitude of what that really means, but in essence it means that *every glorious thing we ever dreamed would occur, when Heaven manifested on Earth,* is now possible. That may seem too good to be true, **but it is absolutely true**, and it is in agreement with all of the prophecies of ages past that foretold of a time when the transformation would take place in the twinkling of an eye.

The problem is we are not recognizing the opportunity at hand because, with our literal interpretation, we thought the prophecy meant that, instantly, our physical reality would change, but that isn't the way transformation works. Initially, in transformation the change occurs in the Realms of Cause. Then, it begins to filter into the consciousness of Humanity, and depending on how effectively we integrate the change in vibration into our daily lives, determines how fast our physical experience and environment reflect the change.

As of January 11, 1992, the shift of the Planet Earth from the "wheel of karma" to the Spiral of Evolution was completed. We are now in alignment with the Solar Light of our God Presence in a way that we have not experienced for aeons of time. The luminous Presence of our Divine Self is poised and ready to take full dominion of our four lower bodies (physical, etheric, mental and emotional). When this transpires, the Light of our God Presence will activate the core of purity pulsating in every electron of our Earthly vehicles. This will expand the Divine Blueprint that was pre-encoded into the RNA-DNA structure of our bodies by our God Presence when we first began our Earthly sojourn. The end result of this Divine Alchemy will be our physical transformation at an atomic cellular level. This means our physical bodies will literally be transfigured into their original Divine Intent, which is Radiant Beauty, Vibrant Health and Eternal Youth. This does not mean just stopping the aging process. It means the reversal of all the degeneration and disease now manifesting in our bodies and the actual physical rejuvenation of every cell and organ.

In order for us to take advantage of this magnificent opportunity, we must reach up in consciousness and strive to clearly perceive just how the Divine unification of our God Self and our physical bodies will occur. Because our physical bodies are severely contaminated with the negativity we have

v

experienced during our lifetimes on Earth, the integration of our Divine Light Body and our physical bodies will be a gradual process. To force our aging, diseased cells into the Light instantaneously would result in physical death. Instead, this process must be gentle and nurturing. Fortunately, we are receiving guidance and assistance from the Illumined Realms of Truth, and the Sacred Knowledge that will enable us to transfigure our bodies as quickly as we can individually withstand, is now being made available.

As you read this book, please ask the Presence of God pulsating in your Heart to envelope you in the Divine Light of Truth, which will enable you to experience the urgency of this message.

We have been told by the Heavenly Realms, time and time again, that this opportunity on Earth is a Cosmic Moment. The expression is "Cosmic Moments come, and Cosmic Moments go." If the Moment is not grasped, the opportunity is missed and may not be presented again for centuries of time. During this Cosmic Moment, we are being given the unparalleled opportunity to reclaim our direction and return this blessed Planet and all life evolving upon Her to the Divine Plan of Heaven on Earth. Everything is in readiness for this to occur. All of the inner work has been accomplished. Now, it is up to those abiding in the physical plane to bring the transformation that has already occurred in the Realms of Cause into the world of form.

Those of you who have magnetized this information into your life have been preparing for thousands of years to be the pioneers who will utilize the Sacred Knowledge and prove the Law through your own physical transformation.

The Divine Fiat of the moment is "As 'I AM' lifted up, all Life is lifted up with me." The pioneers are being asked to apply the tools which are now filtering into the consciousness of all who are willing to reach up into their Divinity and tap the Divine Mind of God. Through the application of this Divine Science of Alchemy, our physical bodies and our physical realities will be transformed. We will, then, be living, tangible proof of the Laws of Transfiguration, and the masses of Humanity will have a Bridge of Light over which they will ascend into their own transfiguration. Without visible proof that we no longer need to experience aging, disease and death, the mass consciousness of Humanity will not trust enough to apply the necessary tools of transformation. Consequently, they will not experience their transformation, and the end result of that sad scenario would be the death of our Planet, instead of Her Ascension into the Light. That, in brief, is the urgency of this message.

Now, the wonderful news is that many, many Illumined Souls have volunteered to be in physical embodiment at this critical moment to apply the Divine Science of Transfiguration and PROVE the Law. It is just a matter of each of us remembering that we have agreed to do what is necessary to transform our bodies into Vibrant Health, Radiant Beauty and Eternal Youth, and, then, doing it. This knowledge is pre-encoded in the memory of our RNA-DNA structures, and when the codes are activated, we will awaken to the Truth of our Divine Mission.

Because the time is short and the task is great, we are being given some super-human assistance to accelerate the activation of our RNA-DNA codes. Through the unification of the efforts of the entire Company of Heaven and the Lightworkers in physical embodiment, a Chalice of Light is being formed that will act as a mighty transformer to step down the Light of God into the physical plane. This will activate the pre-encoded RNA-DNA structures and awaken the pioneers who have volunteered to pave the way for Humanity's transformation. *Anyone* who is willing to apply the tools being given to

Humanity from the Realms of Truth will be given *ALL* of the assistance s/he can absorb to accelerate the transfiguration of their own physical bodies. This opportunity is a gift and a Divine Blessing beyond our greatest expectation. Once this Chalice is formed, it will be secured to pave the way for the masses of Humanity to follow.

This book contains the Sacred Knowledge being shared from on High that will enable us to quickly prove, in tangible, physical reality, the opportunity being presented to Humanity during this Cosmic Moment. The information is the newest, most relevant wisdom available on Earth at this time, regarding physical transformation, and this unique information will enable us to communicate and become cooperative friends with the intelligence of our physical bodies, as these vehicles ascend in vibration into our Light Body of Perfection.

The task we are being asked to accomplish for all Humanity is great, but the rewards will be miraculous.

Take this information into your Heart. See how it resonates for you. If you feel your mission includes the glorious transformation of your own physical body and your physical reality, then respond to your Heart's call and apply the Sacred Knowledge contained in the pages of this book to your daily experience. Then observe your own glorious rebirth.

Thank you for all you do and for all you are.

In deep Love and Gratitude, "I AM",

Patricia Diane Cota-Robles

TABLE OF CONTENTS

CHAPTER
ONE

BECOMING YOUR HOLY CHRIST SELF
THE TRUE MEANING OF
"THE SECOND COMING"

Every world religion has foretold of a coming time when Heaven will manifest on Earth. The prophesies have all indicated that during that reign of Eternal Peace the pain and suffering we are currently going through on Earth will cease to exist. This means that the afflictions of the physical body such as disease, aging, malfunctions, deterioration, deformities, etc., will no longer be part of our Earthly lessons. It also means that every facet of our physical reality will be transformed, and all of the perfection pulsating in the pure land of boundless splendor and infinite Light we call Heaven will become our everyday life experience on Earth.

I think at some level we have all believed, or at least hoped, that these prophesies were true, but we thought that they would happen in some distant, future time, and we believed that they probably wouldn't effect us very much at all. Now, we are hearing, through all levels of consciousness, that the time for Heaven to manifest on Earth is **NOW**. Well, wait a minute. How can that possibly be true? Look at what is going on on this Planet. We are in a hellacious mess. Everything seems to be going wrong. People's lives are in chaos. I've had my counseling patients tell me they feel that Murphy's Law ("if anything can go wrong, it will") is becoming the rule of the day. One patient even said he thought Murphy was an optimist. We are daily witnessing corruption in government and politics, war, failed economic systems, prejudice, intolerance, poverty, disease, pollution, crime, dysfunctional families, overpopulation, substance abuse, famine, floods, hurricanes, tornadoes, volcanic eruptions, earthquakes, plagues, injustice of every conceivable kind, grief, despair, despondency, and total hopelessness. How in the world could anyone be saying this is the time for Heaven to manifest on Earth? We couldn't be further from Heaven if we tried and yet, *that is the information that is pouring forth from the Realms of Illumined Truth.*

In order to comprehend what is actually happening, and in order to give some semblance of sanity to all of this, we need to open our minds, not so far open that our brain falls out, but far enough to let the Light of understanding flow in. Instead of locking into a mind-set of disbelief and professing that the idea of Heaven on Earth is ludicrous or even bizarre, we need to step back to fathom the greater picture.

It is true that things are chaotic on Earth, but interestingly, if we read the prophesies of old, every single one of them indicated things would be just like this before the transformation. What we are now experiencing has been referred to as: the end times; Armageddon; the time of the screaming and the gnashing of teeth; the holocaust; the purge; the latter days; and many other ominous terms. This is the "darkness before the dawn." It is the necessary purging that must take place in order for this Earth and all Her life to Ascend into Her rightful place in our Solar System. This is the Cosmic Moment that was seen by prophets of old. It is the opportunity for Earth's rebirth.

A Cosmic Fiat was issued, and it has been decreed that the moment has arrived for this Planet and all Her life to Ascend into the next spiral of evolution. The problem is that we cannot Ascend into the next evolutionary spiral, which is a spiral of harmony and balance, until we transmute our negative human miscreations. These are the painful expressions of human suffering that we have been struggling with for aeons. Unfortunately, we are so used to our pain that we don't even recognize it as abnormal anymore. Humanity has been so immersed in our humanly created effluvia that we are resigned to our misery. We have numbed ourselves as a survival mechanism, and we are so familiar with our painful lives that they actually seem normal. In order to shock us out of our mass-hypnosis and awaken us from our lethargical trance of indifference, our Father-Mother God had to do something drastic to get our attention

Consequently, for several years now, the Light of God has been increasing on Earth. As this Divine substance enters the core of purity pulsating in the center of every electron of physical form, it has the effect of pushing all of the frequencies of discord and negativity to the surface for purification. This exacerbates our daily challenges, and it creates so much discomfort that we can no longer stuff things down and deny they exist. Through this acceleration of Light, we have become so uncomfortable that we have no other option but to face our trials and strive to find viable solutions for them. Even though this is a little bit scary and sometimes even feels overwhelming, we should be rejoicing for the opportunity being presented to us. After all, we are actually being given the awesome privilege of co-creating Heaven on Earth. What grander mission could we possibly have? And, even more exciting, we are not alone. The entire Company of Heaven is rendering more assistance than has ever been allowed before in the history of time. This absolutely assures that we are going to be able to pull this off. Imagine, you and me working with the Company of Heaven restoring this sweet Earth to Her Divine Birthright. What a humbling honor!

TRANSMUTING THE LOWER HUMAN EGO

The seers of ages past were clearly shown the three mandatory steps Humanity must take in order for Heaven to manifest on Earth.

First: We must become *aware* of the negativity we have created through our abuse of our creative faculties of thought and feeling.

Second: We must *transmute* every electron of our misqualified energy back into Light through the power of Forgiveness and Divine Love.

Third: We must relinquish the grip our lower human ego has on our physical, etheric, mental and emotional bodies and once again *give full dominion of these vehicles to our Holy Christ Self.*

Even though the Cosmic Fiat is ringing through the Universe and we are being given the opportunity to Ascend into the Octaves of Harmony and Balance, our decision to cooperate with this Divine Plan is still subject to our free will choice. If we refuse to *awaken* and accept responsibility for transmuting the negativity we have created on Earth, we will be destined to an act of dissolutionment. Mercifully, through Divine Grace, a plan has been set into motion to try and prevent that tragedy from happening. Through Divine Intervention, our Father-Mother God has been projecting into the consciousness of all Humanity a WAKE-UP CALL. This wake-up call has been entering the atmosphere of Earth in the form of Sacred Fire. The frequency of vibration of this Sacred Fire is reverberating through every atom and molecule of the third dimensional plane of Earth. It is accelerating the vibration of every particle of life, and It is activating the pre-encoded memories recorded as the Divine Blueprint within our RNA-DNA patterns. This activation is reminding us of who we are and why we are here.

In order to perceive these patterns clearly, we must first get our heads above the mud puddle of our suffering. That is why we must first face the challenges now surfacing in our lives to be cleared. We aren't being allowed to be in denial anymore. Too much hangs in the balance. The very survival of Earth is at stake. I know that sounds a little heavy, but it is pure Truth.

The influx of Sacred Solar Fire is accomplishing the **first step** necessary for the creation of Heaven on Earth. It is making Humanity *aware* of the negativity we have created. This awareness, and the pain accompanying it, is motivating us into action. It seems as though we use pain as our most effective motivator. As long as we are comfortable, or more accurately, numb, we will easily stagnate, but in a desperate attempt to alleviate pain, we begin searching for answers and praying for guidance and help. In this uncomfortable state, we refuse to accept the status quo, and we are filled with determination to get out of our pain. As we reach up in consciousness for guidance and direction, the answers and viable solutions begin to flow into our minds.

The Universal Law is "Ask and you shall receive; knock and the door will be opened." As our invocations and prayers ring forth, they open the door to the Divine Mind of God. This door has been closed to the consciousness of Humanity since the "fall of man." The opening of this door gives us access to the Wisdom and Knowledge of the Ages. Contained within this Illumined Truth are all of the answers we have been searching for. This Wisdom is beginning even now to filter into the consciousness of Illumined teachers all over the world. Self-empowerment seminars, workshops, conferences, books and tapes are now available for every level of learning. The teachings reflect the Truth that we are each responsible for creating our own reality, and we are responsible for the condition of the Earth. If one person isn't stating that Truth in a way we can relate to, there are hundreds of other teachers with various ways of expressing the same Truth to choose from.

The Wisdom from the Divine Mind of God is revealing to us the knowledge of the Sacred Fire and how we can invoke this Divine Essence to *transmute* the ills of our lives and the ills of the world through the *power of Forgiveness and Love.* Through the application of the Sacred Fire, the **second step** of our awakening is being accomplished.

The most urgent and **final step** is now in the process of unfolding. This is the step in which we must surrender the hold our lower human ego has on our physical vehicles as we allow our Holy Christ Self to again take full command of our thoughts, words, actions and feelings.

Our lower human ego is a wayward aspect of our intelligence which always functions solely to gratify the physical senses. As we can easily observe, most of our problems are a result of this facet of our consciousness overpowering the influence of our Holy Christ Self, Who only functions in alignment with God's Will. The human ego expresses all extremes of imbalance from dominance and aggression to low self-esteem and cowardice; from greed and selfishness to poverty and lack; from excessive, compulsive addictions to neglect and abuse; from co-dependency to isolation, and on and on. All of the negative experiences manifesting on Earth at this time can be traced back to the poor choices of the lower human ego.

All of the chaos surfacing now is designed to help us recognize the adverse effects we have experienced as a result of the human ego controlling our lives. Hopefully then, we will be inspired to love this perverse personality into the Light so we can relinquish our bodies to their rightful Master. Once we begin to understand this Truth, then we will see that there is a purpose and reason for the painful things appearing on our screen of life. These things are not coming up to punish or destroy us, and they do not prove we are going down the tubes as some people think. They are coming up to expose the human ego for what it truly is and to encourage us to embrace our true God Reality, our Holy Christ Self.

This is merely the *awakening* and *purification* every world religion and prophesy told us would be necessary in order for us to move forward in the Light, thus creating Heaven on Earth.

The scary part of taking our power back from the human ego is that it is the only master we have known for a very long time. It seems as though we will not exist anymore if the only personality we are familiar with ceases to be. The human ego is the aspect of our consciousness that we have usually identified with, and it is who we have believed we really are. In our distorted perception, it feels like we will die if we let the human ego go. Actually, nothing could be further from the Truth. If we will just imagine the human ego as a self-serving, selfish, egotistical, greedy, ignorant brat who has been ravaging our four lower bodies, we will more accurately understand this aspect of our personality, and it will be easier to detach from it. The resistance we have to letting go of the human ego is understandable, since we have been buried in confusion and darkness for so long, but it is really humorous. We are clinging to this wayward human creation who has caused every bit of pain and suffering we have ever experienced. It is responsible for the abusive use of our creative faculties of thought and feeling. It has ignorantly defiled our physical body causing disease, degeneration, aging and even death as we know it. It has led us into poverty, lack and limitation of every conceivable kind. It is the instigator of war, hate, greed, aggression and dominance. Through its obsessive, self-centered consciousness, it has developed into a "me first," dog eat dog, judgmental, prejudiced entity. Just think, this is who we are terrified of letting go of. What a distorted survival mechanism we have developed!

Let's talk about reality. Let's talk about what it really means to let go of the lower human ego and let our Holy Christ Self have command of our four lower bodies. When we begin to truly understand what this means, we will see how absolutely absurd it is for us to be holding onto the human ego so tenaciously.

First of all, let's reflect on who our Holy Christ Self actually is. Our Holy Christ Self is the mediator between God and wo/man. When it was time for us to progress into the experience of third dimensional reality, our God Presence "I AM" projected a reflection of Itself into the slower frequencies of physical matter. This reflection contains the totality of perfection pulsating within our "I AM" Presence, but it is vibrating at a slightly slower frequency. It is held within the radiance of our Three-fold Flame which expresses the Trinity of God: the Divine balance of Love, Wisdom and Power or more often called the Father, Son/Daughter and Holy Spirit (Mother). This reflection of our "I AM" Presence serves as a stepped down transformer. It receives the frequencies of perfection and steps that Divine Light down into a frequency that is compatible with the third dimensional, physical plane. The reflection of our "I AM" Presence is known as our Holy Christ Self, and it is through the process of stepping down the Light of God into a frequency we can utilize in third dimensional reality, that the Christ Self becomes the mediator between God and wo/man.

Before the development of the human ego our Christ Self was the guide and director of our four lower bodies. S/he always remains in constant communion with the Realms of Divinity and continually magnetizes that all-encompassing perfection into the physical plane of Earth. As long as our Holy Christ Self was the director of our thoughts, words, actions and feelings, we experienced only the perfection of Heaven in our Earthly sojourn. The Universal Law of "as above, so below" was our living reality. At that time, our growth and development into self-mastery and fully realized Sons and Daughters of God was relatively rapid. Under the direction of our Holy Christ Self, we experienced a literal Heaven on Earth. There was no such thing as disease, poverty, pain, suffering, war, hate, prejudice, crime or any of the lack and limitation we are currently experiencing. This was the time allegorically referred to as the "Garden of Eden," and it was what God originally intended life on Earth to be like.

It was only after we began experimenting with our thoughts, words, actions and feelings in ways that were conflicting with God's Will that the separate personality of our lower human ego began to develop.

In the original Divine Plan, the purpose for coming into the third dimensional plane of Earth was to give our Holy Christ Self the opportunity to use the creative faculties of thought and feeling to become master of physical energy.

Through the process of thought and feeling, our Holy Christ Self would take unformed primal Light substance and bring it into manifest form as it reflected on the atomic and subatomic particles of physical matter. What we held in our consciousness, we brought into form. The Holy Christ Self, at that time, was in constant communion with the "I AM" Presence and, therefore, the thoughts and feelings It directed through the four lower bodies were always reflecting the perfection of the Heavenly Fourth Dimensional Realms. This enabled the Universal Law of "as above, so below" to become a physical reality. At that point in our evolutionary journey, we were fulfilling our potential as Sons and Daughters of God. We were created in God's image, destined to become co-creators with God, and we used our gift of free will to expand the borders of our Father's Kingdom in the world of form.

For a while, we fulfilled that destiny in perfect Divine Order but, unfortunately, at a particular point in time, Humanity became curious about the commandment of our God Parents. Why should we not partake of the tree of knowledge of good and evil? What will happen? What is evil? Eventually, our curiosity became too much to withstand, and we began experimenting with our thoughts and feelings in ways that were not in alignment with God's Will. The intelligence within our mental body began forming thoughts separately from the directives of the Holy Christ Self. Our emotional body began translating those thoughts into feelings that were not expressed by the Holy Christ Self, and the physical body began acting out the thoughts and feelings without the consent of the Holy Christ Self. The etheric body recorded the distorted patterns of the thoughts and feelings, and the discord began to reflect on the cells and organs of the physical body. This process continued until the four lower bodies actually developed a separate personality that controlled them and operated *in opposition* to the directives of the Holy Christ Self. This is the personality we now refer to as the as the *human ego*.

When the human ego arrogantly took command of our four lower bodies, our Holy Christ Self had no choice but to stand by and watch. Not even the highest aspect of our own Divinity has the authority to interfere with our gift of free will. Gradually, as a merciful activity of life, our Holy Christ Self began withdrawing the Light It was projecting through our four lower bodies from our "I AM" Presence, so that we would have less energy to distort with our negative thoughts and feelings. This caused our Three-fold Flame to become smaller until it eventually shrank to a mere fraction of an inch in our Heart. The tremendous shaft of Light that used to pour through our Seven-fold Planetary Spine from the Twelve-fold Solar Spine of our God Presence became the thin stream of Light we now refer to as the silver cord. This act of mercy saved us from our own self-destruction, but it tragically cut us off to a great degree from our Source.

Our four lower bodies became denser and denser as our negative energy began interpenetrating our cellular structures at an atomic level. This distortion began reflecting as decay, disintegration, disease and death. We fell into denser and denser octaves of matter until the body elemental could no longer rejuvenate the elements of the four lower bodies. This caused the phenomenon we experience now as aging. Instead of the Elemental Vortexes* recharging our cells throughout our lifetime as originally intended, we now come to Earth with charged cells that regenerate effectively for approximately 25 years. Then, just like a battery that is not recharged, the process becomes weaker and weaker until the cells gradually become less vibrant and healthy as time goes on. They finally die altogether in about 70 or 80 years.

This sad state of affairs actually buried us in such a sea of negativity that we were separated in consciousness from our Holy Christ Self; we lost our way, and we forgot about our purpose and reason for being. We forgot about our own Divinity, and we forgot we were Sons and Daughters of God. This deplorable event caused us to look at the physical plane as the only reality. We thought our limited physical body and human ego were all we really were. We began to believe that the pain and suffering existing on Earth were part of God's plan instead of just being the result of misusing our thoughts and feelings. We have been struggling in the muck and mire so long that we don't believe we have a choice anymore. Most of Humanity feels victimized and pitiful. They feel hopeless and desperate. They feel life on Earth is doomed, and there is no

---

*The Elemental Vortexes are discussed in detail in my books *Your Time Is At Hand* and *The Next Step*. (See exercise page 104 in this book.)

turning back from our path of self-destruction. We have bought this lie and lived in this confusion long enough. We have played the absurd game of poverty, disease, hate, war, crime, aging, death and all other forms of limitation as long as we need to. In Ages past, we struggled to get our heads above the mud puddle long enough to see the Light at the end of the tunnel, but we had relatively little success. The Light at the end of the tunnel was often an oncoming train.

What is happening now is that we are mainly focused in our human ego. This state of consciousness is all we have known for aeons of time. It has controlled and manipulated us through fear and the obsessive need to gratify our physical senses. It is volatile and demanding, and it is fighting tooth and nail to stay in control of our four lower bodies. We have been so disconnected from our Holy Christ Self that the human ego is the only thing we believe is real. Even with all its flaws, it seems better than nothing, so we are holding on to it for dear life.

Our Holy Christ Self is a resplendent Being of Light. It is one with our God Presence "I AM", and It has the capability of restoring our Earthly experience to Heaven on Earth. Our Christ Self is anxiously waiting for us to transmute the human ego into the Light so that the rightful Christ Presence can once again guide and direct our physical vehicles. When this occurs, we will no longer experience any of the pain and suffering we endured under the direction of our human ego. This means that all of the perfection of Heaven is available to us if we will only let go of the lower ego.

The reason we are reluctant to do this is because we have been disappointed so very many times in the past. We have developed a fear and a lack of trust that is dominating us now. We are afraid to believe that a Presence as glorious as the Holy Christ Self really exists. Then we are expected to take that belief one step further and accept that the Holy Christ Self is actually who we are, which seems impossible. After all, all of our lives we have been told we were worthless worms in the dust. We have been told we are innately evil sinners, the dregs of creation. How can we possibly be expected to suddenly believe that we are in reality not the scum of the Earth, but in fact, Divine Sons and Daughters of God? This truly takes a quantum leap in awareness, but I promise you, there is not a single pearl of Divine Truth that will be more worth your while to grasp, for once you accept this fact, your eternal freedom is assured.

As I mentioned previously, we are receiving incredible assistance from the Heavenly Realms to enable us to be victorious in our endeavors of transmuting our lower human ego and becoming one with our Holy Christ Self. I would like to share with you some of the work being done at inner and outer levels that will ensure our success in becoming one with our Holy Christ Self and in salvaging this blessed Planet.

PLANET EARTH'S ASCENSION

On January 11, 1992, this precious Planet and all Her Life began the ascent through the "doorway" that unites the third dimensional spiral of physical experience with the Fourth Dimensional spiral of Godly experience. Our Ascension through the doorway into Divinity will take approximately 20 years, until January 11, 2012. This entire Ascension process actually began during the time frame referred to as Harmonic Convergence, August 15-17, 1987, and it is the fulfullment of all of the ancient prophecies of planetary transformation.

We've all known at some level that this Planet would one day regain Her direction and return to Her Divine Intent and Purpose. Unfortunately, because of the adversity manifesting in the world, I don't think we ever really believed it would happen in our lifetime. But, here we are, not only witnessing this glorious event, but actually participating in it. Now, it is beginning to be a little easier to understand what the Divine Beings in the Heavenly Realms meant when They said, "The greatest privilege and honor of ANY Lifestream, regardless of their level of evolution, is physical embodiment on Planet Earth during this Cosmic Moment." We are truly blessed to be on Earth at this time, and it is very important that we realize this is not just a coincidence. We are here because we have been prepared at both inner and outer levels for thousands of years to assist this sweet Earth and all life evolving upon Her into the Octaves of Perfection. Each and every one of us has unique skills, talents and abilities to assist in this process of rebirth. Your particular thread of life is critical to the perfection of the overall tapestry of transformation being woven into the plan of creation. Not another soul possesses your specific expertise in exactly the same way you do. You are an imperative part of the plan, and so is every other particle of life on Earth.

As we begin to tap the wisdom and knowledge of our Divine Plan, which is clearly recorded in the Flame of Divinity pulsating in our Hearts, we begin to recognize the magnitude of what is happening on Earth. Earth is returning to her Divine Heritage. Heaven on Earth (as above, so below) was the original plan for this physical, third dimensional experience. The "fall of man" was a human creation that resulted in disease, poverty, war, hate, suffering, aging, destructive weather conditions, decay, pollution, death and all other forms of grossly misqualified energy. None of these distorted experiences was ever intended by God to be part of our Earthly lessons. When we think of changing these painful conditions, it really seems like an impossible task. Imagine eliminating such things as poverty, disease, aging, hate, war and death. The prospect seems insurmountable, but that is part of the illusion of our fallen perception. Actually, everything that exists in any realm of creation is merely a frequency of energy, vibration and consciousness. The only difference between the Heavenly Octaves of ecstasy and bliss and the hellish octaves of anguish and misery is the frequency of vibration and consciousness the energy in that particular octave is pulsating in. The Heavenly

Octaves vibrate at a high frequency of Harmony and Balance. The hellish frequencies on Earth vibrate at a very low frequency of discord and imbalance. If we will just contemplate that for a moment, we will begin to realize how awesomely simple transformation really is. In order to change all of the pain and suffering on Earth, ALL WE HAVE TO DO IS RAISE THE VIBRATION OF ENERGY AND CONSCIOUSNESS.

All of the suffering on Earth is the result of the *descent* in energy, vibration and consciousness. Now, we are reversing this process, and all transformation will be the result of the ascension of energy, vibration and consciousness.

> LOVE is the Ascension of hate.
> PEACE is the Ascension of war.
> PROSPERITY is the Ascension of poverty.
> HEALTH is the Ascension of disease.
> HAPPINESS is the Ascension of sadness.
> SUCCESS is the Ascension of failure.
> FRIENDSHIP is the Ascension of loneliness.
> PURPOSE is the Ascension of hopelessness.
> TRUTH is the Ascension of ignorance.
> FORGIVENESS is the Ascension of judgment.
> JUSTICE is the Ascension of injustice.
> FREEDOM is the Ascension of oppression.
> LIBERTY is the Ascension of domination.
> PLENTY is the Ascension of lack.
> TOLERANCE is the Ascension of prejudice.
> ACCEPTANCE is the Ascension of criticism.
> CHRIST is the Ascension of human ego.
> HEAVEN is the Ascension of hell.

Can we possibly grasp the significance of what this really means? We don't have to do battle with every negative challenge occurring on Earth. We need only to invoke the Light and increase the vibratory frequency of energy and consciousness. The negative circumstances on Earth cannot exist in the frequency of Harmony. DARKNESS CANNOT EXIST IN THE PRESENCE OF LIGHT.

I know this may sound too good to be true and even a little bit like a cop-out, but all we have to do is look at what changes have taken place since the vibratory rate of the Planet began accelerating on Harmonic Convergence in 1987.

We were told initially, by the Realms of Illumined Truth, that Harmonic Convergence was the beginning impulse of a 25 year acceleration that would move this Planet from the third dimensional frequencies of physical experience into the more rarified frequencies of Fourth Dimensional Solar experience. It was explained that the first phase of the acceleration would take approximately five years and would involve an intense purging of all life evolving on Earth. Any area of existence that was not based in integrity and reverence for life would be pushed to the surface for observation and purification. This occurred individually and collectively for all life evolving on Earth. Since Harmonic Convergence, we have experienced the purging of the stock market, savings and loan companies, political figures, religious figures, our own personal lives and experiences, the fall of Communism, the Berlin Wall, the Soviet Union, and Apartheid. We have experienced Desert Storm, Middle East peace talks and worldwide efforts to curb pollution and the destruction of the rain forests, wildlife and Mother Earth. We have also experienced an awakening that is revealing to us clearly the oneness of all life, the family of Humanity and the power of global group endeavors. The past few years have truly been a paradox; on one level, probably the most challenging we have ever experienced, and on another level, the most glorious and hopeful.

At the time of Harmonic Convergence, we were told the first five years would be very difficult and tumultuous, but following that, there would be an upward shift in vibration that would move our entire Solar system into frequencies of greater Harmony and Balance, thus rendering the next 20 years easier and more miraculous.

The Solar Eclipse of July 11, 1991, and the corresponding inbreath of January 11, 1992, did indeed move us into frequencies of Solar Light beyond anything we have ever experienced.* Now it is our responsibility to utilize that Light effectively to assist in the 20 year process of transformation now upon us.

On January 11, 1992, we moved into alignment with the Twelve-fold Solar spine of our "I AM" Presence, and our dear Planet Earth moved into alignment with Her Solar Spine (axis), as well. Now, we are on a brand new Solar Spiral, and the Sun Cycles we have utilized each month will be reflecting to us unprecedented frequencies of the Twelve-fold Solar Aspect of Deity. These frequencies will increase daily and hourly as we focus our attention on them, and they will offer us an opportunity to transform our physical reality into LIMITLESS PHYSICAL PERFECTION. This is a project we will be accepting as Lightworkers. We will be working to actually transform our physical experiences and our physical bodies into the perfection that was originally our Divine Plan.

We have moved through the "doorway," and we are now Ascending daily and hourly into higher frequencies of Harmony and Balance. As you know, the Earth is in the midst of a unique experiment. Never before has a planet so immersed in negativity been given an opportunity to Ascend into the Light so quickly. This is a dispensation of God's omnipotent mercy and compassion. It is an expression of pure Divine Love.

---

*This Ascension in vibration was popularly referred to as "moving through the doorway of the 11:11." This described in a nutshell the window of opportunity that was opened between July 11, 1991, and January 11, 1992 .

As is the case with all experiments, there are many variables that will determine the outcome. I know many people were feeling that once we made the shift on January 11, 1992, into higher octaves of Harmony, all of our challenges would cease. In Truth, we are now aligned with the Solar Light of our God Presence in a way that we have not been since the "fall of man" aeons ago. Therefore, we do have the ability to transcend the pain of our Earthly experience and actually create Heaven on Earth in our daily lives *right here and right now*. The problem is that we are having a great deal of trouble accepting that Truth.

When a major shift in vibration like the one we've experienced occurs, not even the Heavenly Realms know exactly how it is going to affect every particle of life. Each person will be affected differently, depending on the very individual experiences they are going through in their Earthly sojourn. No two people have exactly the same life path, and consequently, we will each experience the changes in a unique way. The feedback I am getting indicates people are going through the gamut of experiences. Some people feel things have actually gotten worse in their lives; others feel confused and seem to be experiencing an unfounded sense of anger, even rage. On the other extreme, some feel "blissed out," spacey and high to the point of not being able to concentrate on their work. Maybe you've heard the expression, "They're so Heavenly, they're no Earthly good."

Other people are feeling more subtle changes; more inner peace, more confidence, more success in their endeavors, more hope, generally happier, less anxious, less stressed out, less fearful. Regardless of what the individual experience may be, I haven't spoken to anyone who hasn't experienced some sort of change.

The important thing for each of us to do is to continually go within and ask our Higher Selves to give us clarity and discernment. Ask to have revealed to you just exactly what has taken place, and how it is going to affect you personally.

It is imperative that we effectively integrate the new frequencies of the Solar Fires of Creation that are pouring through our Solar Spines now. How well these energies are integrated will set the tone for the next 20 years, as we journey into the Fourth Dimension.

The more we draw these Sacred Aspects of Deity through our beings, the higher our vibratory rate will become. This will help us greatly to lift out of the pain and confusion. When we lift out of the emotional trauma of our daily lives, we will begin to recognize viable solutions and other constructive options for handling situations that we can't see when we are immersed in pain and fear. Remember, we have been told by the Realms of Truth that Limitless Physical Perfection is now available to ALL life evolving on Earth. This means not only the Transformation of our physical bodies, but also our physical realities which include relationships, finances, jobs, health, environment and all the rest of our physical experiences.

Now that our Seven-fold Planetary Spine has Ascended into the embrace of our Twelve-fold Solar Spine, the Aspect of Deity that is projected into the Earth each month through the normal Sun Cycles has been greatly intensified. If we will lift up in consciousness and invoke the Divine Qualities of the Sun Cycles through us each month, it will help us beyond measure to integrate the new energies effectively.

It seems the more people I talk to, the more obvious it becomes that each and every one of us is creating our own experience from the accelerated flow of energy that began on January 11, 1992. I know it has always been true that we create our own realities, but never before have I seen such extreme diversity appearing in people's lives so quickly. It is as though we are living in a hologram. A hologram is described as a picture that is given a multidimensional image when illuminated with coherent light.

Our experience is dependent upon:
1. Where we focus our attention;
2 What energies we have individually volunteered to lift up with us as we Ascend into the Light;
3. What learning experiences and lessons we are completing;
4. How easily we are letting go of "old baggage"; and
5. How consistently we are envisioning our glorious Transformation.

If we observe our lives through one angle of the hologram, we see the "old Earth" with all of its flaws and limitations. If we change our perspective of the hologram, we observe the "new Earth" with all its resplendent beauty and potential for limitless perfection.

In numerology the number 1 1 1 is the number of perfection. On January 11, (1-11) we began our Ascent through the doorway of 11:11. The number 11:11 is an inner code symbolizing the Ascent toward oneness. All of the Sacred Geometry for inner and outer world Transformation is in place. Now, it is up to each of us to empower the vision and experience of the "new Earth" by vigilantly focusing the full power of our attention on the Divine Blueprint for our lives. This includes the most magnificent image of what our lives will be when Heaven has manifested permanently on Earth. There will be vibrant health, eternal youth, prosperity, peace, love, cooperation, reverence for all life, and abounding joy and happiness. Pain, suffering, disease, war, hunger, homelessness, poverty, loneliness, etc., will no longer exist. Eventually, this will manifest for every particle of life on Earth, but what we must realize is that it is available to us HERE AND NOW, according to our ACCEPTANCE. We don't have to wait any longer.

At this very moment, your life is reflecting what you believe to be true about yourself. The ironic thing is we usually think the opposite is happening. We think that the reason we believe we are poor is because we don't have any money. We think the reason we believe we are not loveable is because nobody loves us. We think the reason we believe we are failures is because we are not succeeding. We think the reason we believe we are unhappy is because we are not experiencing happiness. That seems perfectly logical. We evaluate what is going on in our lives, and we simply judge the facts...I'm lonely. I'm poor. I'm a failure. I'm unhappy. I'm sick. The problem is, even though it seems like plain common sense to evaluate our lives in that manner, that interpretation is absolutely wrong.

In order for us to be poor, we must *first* have a belief system based in the poverty consciousness of lack and limitation. In order for us to be without loving relationships, we must *first* believe we are unlovable. In order for us to be unsuccessful, we must *first* believe we are failures. In order for us to be unhappy, we must *first* believe we don't deserve happiness.

If you will only stretch your understanding to grasp the magnitude of this simple Truth, you will realize that you have created your present life situation by believing what you do about yourself and will then know you have the ability to improve your life by correcting your belief systems and your self-esteem.

Every single day your life is merely reflecting what you believe to be true about yourself. It is reflecting your sense of identity, your self-esteem, your self-worth, your self-respect and your personal opinions about yourself.

The concepts and attitudes we have about ourselves began forming at the moment of our conception. Even as we were being molded in our mother's womb, we were making judgments about our experiences. Am I wanted? Am I loved? Is my mother happy? Is she sad? Is she angry? Is she afraid? We heard sounds and sensed emotions. We felt when she was peaceful, and we knew when she was stressed. Then we went through the throes of the birthing process into the glaring light and clamor of the outer world. Our senses were activated, and we became miniature receiving circuits. We began recording every single experience and interpreting what it meant through our limited perception. If we were nurtured and loved, we interpreted that to mean we were valuable. If we were neglected or abused, we interpreted that to mean we were not valuable. From that initial impression, we began to form a sense of identity about ourselves, and day by day that identity developed according to our experiences.

Now, we are being given an opportunity to take a quantum leap out of the distorted belief of unworthiness and limitation into the limitless perfection of the "new Earth." And, believe it or not, we can do it by changing the angle of our perception and viewing the hologram through the eyes of our Holy Christ Self, who always knows *the truth of who we are, instead of the illusion of who we've become.*

One of the most wonderful, miraculous things that has occurred is that we have been brought into alignment once again with our Holy Christ Self. We have been struggling to heal our self-inflected separation from this part of our consciousness since the "fall of man" aeons ago. All we have to do now is ALLOW this Divine Presence to take command of our four lower bodies and our thoughts, words, actions and feelings, and S/He will guide us unerringly through the most glorious Transformation we could ever envision.

In order for us to give our Holy Christ Self full dominion over our lives, we need to be constantly alert and really practice the Presence of God daily and hourly. When old patterns or challenges occur in our lives, instead of just responding out of our old reflexes, we need to say, *"Wait a minute, that is not who I am anymore. I don't have to act out of the old habit; I have a choice. 'I AM' my Holy Christ Self, and I now respond according to the highest good for all concerned. I see constructive, viable solutions. I respect myself and respond as the Holy Christ Self 'I AM'."*

As we continually practice being our Holy Christ Self, that Illumined Presence will be integrated through our four lower bodies (physical, etheric, mental and emotional) at an atomic cellular level. Then, our bodies will begin to outpicture the perfection of this Being of Light, and we will be physically Transformed.

One day we won't have to work so hard to hold our attention on the vision of perfection. One day soon, it will be such a powerful part of our consciousness that perfection is all we will experience.

When that occurs, it will be hard for us to fathom how we could have allowed the pain and suffering on Earth to be part of our consciousness for so long. The distorted patterns of disease, poverty, war, aging, hate, etc., will be so unfamiliar to us that they will seem as ludicrous and unbelievable as the concept of Heaven on Earth seems to some people now.

Your Holy Christ Self is here now;
ACCEPT IT!
Transformation is available to you now;
ACCEPT IT!
You can manifest limitless physical perfection now;
ACCEPT IT!
The Earth's Ascension into Eternal Light has begun;
ACCEPT IT!
You are a co-creator of Heaven on Earth;
ACCEPT IT!

ACCEPTING OUR NEW REALITY

During the fall, we were separated from the awareness of our Holy Christ Selves so completely that we came to accept the limited physical plane of pain and suffering as the only reality. No matter how hard we tried, it was practically impossible for us to raise ourselves up out of the darkness for any sustained length of time. Consequently, we stumbled and fell time and time again. Our progress was painfully slow, and poverty, disease, war, hate, anger, corruption, deceit and all manner of negative behavior became the order of the day on Earth. It is truly a miracle that we survived. But we have survived, and not only have we survived, we have moved through the doorway and placed our feet firmly on the path of our *God Victorious Ascension into the Light.*

The important thing now is for us to accept this *Divine Truth* and begin living our lives out of the new reality.

We are such creatures of habit that we often act out of old familiar patterns long after the pattern has become obsolete. It is common knowledge that obese people who lose weight still think and act out patterns of obesity. Even though they are thin, the old obsolete patterns of obesity, being energized by their belief system, causes them to re-create their overweight condition. Many times, poor people who come into a lot of money unexpectedly do not change their poverty consciousness and end up being poor again in a very short time. There is a theory that if all of the money in the world was divided evenly among all of the people, in five years all of the rich people would be rich again, and all of the poor people would be poor again. That would be the direct result of acting out of old, obsolete patterns and belief systems.

People who believe they are worthless or failures are, every now and then, presented with an opportunity to turn their lives around and really succeed. Too many times, unfortunately, they hold onto the old obsolete patterns and sabotage themselves, thus fulfilling their belief in failure.

We must be careful not to do the same thing now. We have completed a quantum leap in frequency and vibration. This Divine Activity of Light was what is known as a Cosmic Inbreath of our Father-Mother God. The result of this unique opportunity was the straightening of the Spiritual Axis of Earth and the beginning of the Ascent of the Blessed Planet Earth and all Her life into the octaves of Harmony and Balance. We are now in alignment to receive the Divine Light of our Holy Christ Selves in a way that we have not been able to for aeons of time. This literally means that THE STRUGGLE IS OVER!!! We can now tangibly BE our Christ Presence. We no longer have to blindly grope in the darkness for a shred of hope, a glimmer of Light. We can now be the Sons and Daughters of God that we are destined to be, the *Christ* grown to full stature. This is the fulfillment of the prophecies of old, proclaiming the Second Coming of the Christ. This is the moment of the Earth's rebirth into Her resplendent Glory and Light. She is donning Her Seamless Garment of Light, and you and I are being given the awesome privilege of assisting Humanity through the birthing process.

We must stop and grasp the magnitude of this Cosmic Moment. Our responsibility is unparalleled. We have been given the opportunity to be Lightbearers in the past, but never has so much been at stake. Everything is being accelerated. We are experiencing a collapsing of time as we Ascend into the Fourth Dimensional octaves, where time and space cease to exist. If we are still trying to function in linear time, we feel rushed and as though the days are flying by. We have the false impression that we don't have enough time to accomplish what we need to get done. We feel stressed out, hassled and anxious. This is an old obsolete pattern of the Earth, prior to our Ascension on January 11th. It is no longer applicable in our everyday lives.

In order for us to integrate the frequencies of the Earth's new garment of resplendent beauty into the atomic cellular structure of physical matter, truly manifesting Heaven on Earth, we need to stop acting out of old obsolete patterns and move into the reality of Limitless Physical Perfection. This will deeply affect every facet of our lives.

Each time one of us achieves mastery over our physical reality, we expand the Highway of Light into the Octaves of Perfection, creating a wider passage for the rest of Humanity. That is our most important service at this time.

It is not enough to intellectually know about the possibility of Limitless Physical Perfection; we must now accomplish it through every fiber of our beings. I know this sounds like a monumental task, but that is only if we are operating out of our old obsolete belief systems. If we have accepted the new physical reality of Heaven on Earth, our Transformation is a slight adjustment in our attitude.

In the old age, we needed to work through every learning experience. We needed to feel it, live it, experience it, analyze it, rehash it and walk through it in order to learn the lesson and Transmute it. In this New Age, we need merely to release it into the Violet Flame of Forgiveness, flood it with the Pink Flame of Divine Love and invoke the Emerald Green Flame of Illumined Truth to reveal to us the lesson contained within the experience.

In the old age, every bit of progress was achieved through rigorous discipline and painstaking patience. In the New Age, we realize, with great joy and relief, that Divinity is incredibly SIMPLE. We Ascend into Christ Consciousness not through self-flagellation, self-deprivation, guilt, shame, self-denial and all other states of oppressive consciousness, but by simply *accepting* our Divine birthright as a Son or Daughter of God. I know from our old obsolete patterns this seems too good to be true, but the fact is *it is true,* and all we have to do to prove it is *do it.*

ACCEPTING OUR DIVINE BIRTHRIGHT
AS A CHILD OF GOD . . .
BECOMING THE CHRIST

We all have one behavior pattern or another that was developed in the old age that is no longer appropriate as we manifest our full potential as our Holy Christ Selves. Often these patterns are so ingrained and so much a part of who we've accepted ourselves to be that we can't imagine being without them. Even if they are self-destructive, at least they are familiar, and we know what to expect from them. These patterns can be obsessive-compulsive habits and addictions, co-dependency, low self-esteem, poverty, disease, failure, fear, loneliness, anger, abuse, hate, depression, boredom, frustration, stress, anxiety, dysfunctional relationships, and on and on ad infinitum.

In the new frequencies of Harmony and Balance the Earth is now abiding in, we no longer need to maintain our limited sense of identity by holding on to self-defeating habits and beliefs. We need to identify with the *Truth* of who we are, a *Child of God*, and as we act out of that sense of identity, we will become the full manifestation of our Holy Christ Selves.

In order for this to happen, all we have to do is accept it, but because we are such creatures of struggle and habit, that seems very hard to do. Accepting our true God Reality is very easy, but it does take the consistent focus of our attention. We don't have to do battle with all the old patterns; we just need to accept that that is no longer who we are.

Visualization

Envision yourself walking through magnificent massive Golden Doors. You are passing from the old age of lack and limitation into the Glorious Golden Age of Limitless Physical

Perfection. The doors gently close behind you, and all of the dysfunctional, negative patterns of the "old you" are left behind. God's infinite power of Transmutation blazes in, through and around all of the discordant thoughtforms, beliefs and behavior patterns of the old age, and they are instantly Transmuted by the Violet Flame of Forgiveness.

The residue of the old age on the other side of the Golden Doors is now flooded with the Pink Flame of God's Divine Love.

The Emerald Green Flame of Illumined Truth now bathes every electron of your four lower bodies, and the lesson and solution of every experience of the old age is clearly recorded in your etheric records for all time. This Wisdom is permanently available, ready to surface into your conscious mind whenever you need to remember during the remainder of your Earthly sojourn.

You now step forward into the New Earth, and you perceive Her new garment...the Pure Land of Boundless Splendor and Infinite Light. You realize Her rebirth has been God Victorious, and you feel Her abounding Joy.

You see that every man, woman and child is expressing the reality of their true selves...the Christ grown to full stature. Every Elemental Being of the nature kingdom is rejoicing in co-operative service with Humanity. You observe the Angelic Kingdom as these glorious Beings project the feeling nature of God into the world of form. At last, Humanity, Elementals and Angels walk hand-in-hand, expressing a Reverence for all Life, as they emulate the Cosmic Law, "As Above, so Below."

The luminous presence of your Holy Christ Self envelopes your physical, etheric, mental and emotional bodies. Your Immortal Victorious Three-fold Flame embraces these vehicles and lifts them into the Light. You are now resonating within what has been referred to as your Light Body, and you experience the Limitless Physical Perfection of all your vehicles.

You are radiantly beautiful, eternally youthful, vibrantly healthy, slim, firm, flawless form. You are outpicturing the perfection of your Holy Christ Self.

You remember deep within your Heart the Truth of your Divinity. Regardless of how long you have been in your self-imposed exile from your Holy Christ Self, this reunion feels warmly familiar. Your Heart opens, and you are flooded with the Love and Gratitude of your God Presence. Your self-inflicted separation from your true God Reality is Healed once and for all. Now, in the embrace of your Holy Christ Self, you hear from the very core of your Being...Welcome Home, My Beloved Child.

The control your lower human ego had over your four lower bodies is instantly relinquished, and that wayward aspect of your personality Ascends into the Light.

Your Holy Christ Self takes full dominion of your thoughts, words, feelings, memories and actions. You are now the Christ grown to full stature, and you affirm that reality:

"I AM" the Christ grown to full stature. *(Three times)*

Occasionally, an old obsolete behavior pattern may try to surface out of habit, and you need to remember that is no longer who you are.

If an old addiction or pattern surfaces, simply command:

In the full power of my God Presence "I AM" ...

1.* ADDICTION, be still, you have no power. **"I AM" in control here, and "I AM" the limitless perfection of my Holy Christ Self** *now* **made manifest and eternally sustained by Grace.**

"I AM" filled with God's ...

2.* SATISFACTION, and I command all frequencies contrary to that into the Light for instant Transmutation.

My Holy Christ Self seals me in the embrace of Divine Love, and "I AM" now eternally FREE!

*Insert the appropriate words into the blanks with the asterisk.

*1.		*2.	
	POVERTY		GOD'S ABUNDANCE
	DISEASE		GOD'S VIBRANT HEALTH
	FEAR		GOD'S PEACE
	HATE		GOD'S LOVE
	SADNESS		GOD'S HAPPINESS
	LONELINESS		GOD'S FRIENDSHIP
	FAILURE		GOD'S SUCCESS
	IGNORANCE		GOD'S TRUTH
	HUMAN EGO		GOD'S CHRIST PRESENCE
	JUDGMENT		GOD'S ACCEPTANCE
	RESENTMENT		GOD'S FORGIVENESS
	PREJUDICE		GOD'S TOLERANCE
	GRIEF		GOD'S JOY
	UNWORTHINESS		GOD'S HIGH SELF-ESTEEM
	GLUTTONY		GOD'S INNER PEACE
	ANXIETY		GOD'S FULFILLMENT
	STRESS		GOD'S SERENITY
	ANGER		GOD'S CALM

Or any other obsolete behavior pattern from the old age that might surface.

As little behaviors manifest throughout the day that do not reflect the perfection of your Holy Christ Self, remind yourself, *"No, that was the old me; I no longer have to behave that way. As the Christ, I choose to behave this new positive way instead."* Then, respond the way you intuitively feel the empowered presence of Christ would.

The more you ask yourself, *"How would my Holy Christ Self respond in this situation?"*, the more you will tune into that state of your own consciousness, and the easier it will be for your Christ Presence to act through you.

Day by day, the New Earth will become more real and tangible to you. You will realize that every moment is sacred, and you will begin to experience everything you do with a new awareness of Reverence. The things that used to seem bothersome or mundane will take on a deeper sense of purpose. Trivial activities will become meaningful opportunities instead of just annoyances. Have fun with this. Regardless of what you are doing or who you are interacting with, find a way to add to the Light of the world through the experience.

Your Holy Christ Self is a buoyant, joyous Being of Light. When you allow this aspect of your consciousness to take full command of your thoughts, words, actions and feelings, you will live a life of abounding Happiness.

THE SUMMER OF '92

The Summer of 1992 was an experience of God Victorious Accomplishment beyond anything this blessed Planet and Her evolving lifestreams have ever witnessed. It was truly a multi-dimensional activity of Light that deeply affected every particle of life on Earth. None of us will ever be the same again, and whether we participated in the life transforming events consciously or unconsciously, we will reap the benefits for all Eternity.

Preparation for that glorious span of time had been orches-
trated by the unified efforts of Heaven and Earth for literally
thousands of years. Even though the Divine Plan on Earth is
always subject to the free will choices of Humanity, it was
perceived aeons ago that, during the Cosmic Moment of the
Summer of 1992, there would be millions of awakened souls
in embodiment who would be capable of magnetizing the Light
of God into the physical plane of Earth with enough power to
propel this Planet out of the darkness into the Light.

Many accelerations of vibration have taken place on Earth
over the past few years. Some are very well known, such as
World Healing Day, Harmonic Convergence, Earth Link, Star
Link, Earth Day, Time Warp and Ascending through the
Doorway of the 11:11. Many, many additional accelerations
also took place that were not as globally publicized but were
equally transformational. Each of these accelerations lifted
Humanity and all life evolving on Earth up an octave in
vibration out of the oppressive frequencies of the sea of
negativity that surrounds this Planet. Step by step, we have
moved into frequencies of Light that vibrate with more Divine
Qualities of Harmony and Balance. This gradual Ascension has
had the effect of softening our Hearts and awakening our minds
to the realization of the Oneness of all Life. It has literally
healed our self-inflicted separation from our God Presence "I
AM" and has brought us into alignment with the Divine
mediator between God and Humanity, our Holy Christ Self.

This Divine Presence, and not our lower human ego, is the
true master of our Earth vehicles--our physical, etheric, mental
and emotional bodies.

Our lower human ego usurped the control of these Earthly
bodies from our Holy Christ Self when it began to abuse our gift
of free will by using these vehicles strictly to fulfill the
gratification of the physical senses. When this wayward aspect
of our consciousness took dominion of our bodies away from

their true authority, it wreaked havoc in the elemental sub-stance that comprised these vehicles. The atomic cellular structure became cloaked in negativity and contaminated with all manner of human excess. Our bodies, which were originally created to be radiant and beautiful, began to disintegrate and become aged and diseased. This negativity began to reflect on the elemental substance of the environment surrounding us as well, and gradually the body of Mother Earth also experienced contamination, deterioration and disease.

The dominance of the lower human ego in the physical plane is what history has referred to as the "fall of man," and truly, that fall into physical gratification and excess is the cornerstone of all of the problems now manifesting on this Planet. It is the initial cause of aging, disease and even death as we know it now. It is also the cause of greed, selfishness, aggression, corruption, domination, oppression, manipulation and deception. These destructive character traits have effec-tively led to war, hate, poverty, fear, self-destruction, pollu-tion, crime, abuse of human rights, animal rights and civil rights--in essence, all of our Earthly woes.

In order for this carnage to cease, it is critical that we relinquish the control our lower human ego has over our bodies and, once again, allow our physical, etheric, mental and emotional vehicles to function under the full dominion of our Holy Christ Self.

Through the unparalleled healing that took place during the Summer of '92, we are in a position, as never before, to raise our Earthly bodies into the loving embrace of our true God Reality. It is really impossible for us to comprehend with our finite minds the magnitude of just what all this means, but we are now experiencing the initial impulse of PERMANENT Planetary Transformation. We are co-creating the Ascension of this sweet Earth into Her Divine birthright of Heaven on Earth. This, literally, means the transformation of all physical matter at an atomic cellular level. It involves the activation of the pre-encoded memories contained within the RNA-DNA patterns of all living substance. These memories reflect the original Divine intent of all manifest form in the third dimensional plane. This Divine intent is LIMITLESS PHYSICAL PERFECTION.

What this means to human beings is eternal youth, vibrant health, radiant beauty, prosperity, happiness and fulfillment in every facet of our physical existence. What it means to the nature kingdom is purification, beauty, harmony, balance and loving cooperation with Humanity. LIMITLESS PHYSICAL PERFECTION also means the wisdom and enlightenment of Oneness and the Reverence for all Life.

The First Earth Summit

One of the most devastating results of the "fall of man" was the schism that was formed between the Human Kingdom and the Elemental Kingdom on Earth. In the original Divine Plan, Humanity, Elementals and Angels walked hand-in-hand in conscious cooperation. After the "fall," we lost the ability to commune with the Elementals and Angels because we were buried in darkness. We perceived the nature kingdom to be void of intelligence. Consequently, the lower human ego obsessively abused the elements of Earth for its personal gain. This brought us to the brink of self-destruction. The degrading plight of Humanity and the abominable pollution of Mother Earth clearly reflect the war that has been going on between Humanity and the Elements. Now, one of the most critical factors of Planetary Transformation is the healing of the abyss separating the two kingdoms. Every electron of the physical plane is comprised of Elemental substance: earth, air, water, fire and ether. There is no way that we can transform physical matter without the cooperation of the Elemental Kingdom. So, needless to say, our primary goal is to heal the battle going on between the Nature Kingdom and Humanity, if we are going to regain our original path and restore the physical plane to Heaven on Earth.

Once this healing has occurred and we are working in loving cooperation with the intelligence of our physical bodies and the intelligence of the environment of Earth, we will experience the restoration and rejuvenation of our bodies and the transformation of the body of Mother Earth as well.

Since the human ego is very manipulative and very recalcitrant, we had to actually bring the Earth to the brink of dissolution in order to get our attention. Only after our air was polluted, our water putrified, our Earth plagued with global warming, ozone depletion, floods, famines, deforestation, animal extinction, over-population, poverty, bizarre weather changes, disease, aging and death, did we finally say..."Wait a minute, I think something is wrong here."

When that realization finally registered in our conscious minds, we took the first step toward reversing our downward spiral into oblivion. Our awareness that the outrageous behavior of our obsessive, greedy human egos had brought the Earth and all Her life to the threshold of extinction ultimately shocked us sufficiently to motivate us into action. Awakening souls began to seek viable solutions to the problems manifesting on Earth. It became very clear that our challenges were monumental, and it would take the unified efforts of Humanity to change our current direction of ruination and reclaim our Divine Path of co-creating Heaven on Earth.

Individuals and groups began to connect, once again, with the Earth. They sought out the indigenous people of Earth who had not lost the ability to commune with the Elementals, and they began to invoke the Light of God through Sacred Ceremonies of Love and Forgiveness. The Elemental Kingdom began to cautiously observe the Lightworkers' efforts, and at first very skeptically, watched and wondered. It was obvious that we had rendered asunder every bit of trust the Elementals had for us, and that trust was not going to be restored easily. Fortunately, the awakened souls realized the extreme degree of abuse we had inflicted upon the Elementals and continued to persevere. Ever so slowly, the Elementals began to trust the sincere desire of the Lightworkers to heal the separation between the Elementals and themselves, and the desire, once again, to unite in cooperative service to Mother Earth. This sincere desire to heal and reunite, arising in the Hearts of Humanity and Elementals, attracted the attention of the entire Company of Heaven. The unified Heart call of Humanity and Elementals invoked assistance from the Realms of Illumined Truth, and the Heavenly response set a plan into motion to **permanently heal** the schism between Human Beings and Elemental Beings. The Clarion Call rang through the Universe and activated within the Hearts and minds of Humanity the need to set our petty differences aside and come together as a unified force with the common goal of healing the Earth.

   The Lifestreams already aligned with the environment began to redouble their efforts, and a Divine Blueprint for an outer world activity of Light that had never before been attempted began to form in the ethers. This blueprint filtered into the consciousness of world leaders and lay people alike. The organization that symbolizes global unification, the United Nations, chose to accept the responsibility of organizing this glorius event. Plans were set into motion, and the very first **Earth Summit** began to manifest. The United Nations decided to call this sacred conclave *The United Nations Conference on Environment and Development* (UNCED). It was scheduled to be held in Rio de Janeiro, Brazil, June 1-14, 1992.

   Brazil, interestingly, symbolizes the paradox going on in both Humanity and the Elementals. Rio de Janeiro is a beautiful city of approximately nine million people. It clearly reflects all of Humanity's ills: pollution, dire poverty, homelessness, abandoned children, deforestation, inequality, corruption, despair, disease, crime, perversion, substance abuse, etc. Yet, in the midst of Humanity's darkness, there is a blazing Light of beauty and wonder. There is a Spiritual core of awakened souls that hold tenaciously to the knowledge that we truly have a choice. They understand that we have created our present plight, and we alone can change it. They know of their own Divinity, and they are determined to be God in Action on Earth.

The Elementals in Brazil are some of the most exquisite on the Planet. The shimmering waters and tropical rain forests sustain an awe-inspiring variety of lifeforms. The mountains, valleys, skies and beaches are filled with splendor.

Ironically, it was because of the extremes existing in Brazil that this location was chosen for the first Earth Summit. What better place to draw the attention of the world as we focus on what the lower human ego has done to destroy Mother Earth and what Divine Humanity can now do to heal Her.

For two years, the world prepared at both inner and outer levels for the largest gathering of world leaders and non-governmental organizations ever known in the history of time. The Earth Summit was truly a multidimensional activity of Light.

During the mystical month of May preceding the Earth Summit, the Feminine Polarity of God, known to us most commonly as the Holy Spirit, increased in vibration and power on Earth. This Feminine essence of Divine Love has always been the sustaining force behind the Elemental Kingdom. That is why we refer to the elements as *Mother* Nature and *Mother* Earth. As the embrace of the Holy Spirit caressed the abused bodies of the Elementals on Earth, they began to soften their Hearts toward their Earthly adversaries, the Human Beings. This nurturing Mother's Love helped prepare them for the healing that was to take place during the Earth Summit and enabled the Elementals to contemplate Humanity's remorse and our plea for forgiveness. In order for the Elemental Kingdom to believe we were really serious about wanting to heal the atrocities we have perpetrated upon them, we needed to join together in an obvious demonstration. The Earth Summit was the vehicle designed to prove to all the world, at both inner and outer levels, that at long last, Humanity has finally recognized our reponsibility as stewards of the Earth.

For the first time ever, 176 world leaders came together for a common cause: the healing of the Earth. Each leader had his own agenda and his own ideas on how the healing would be accomplished, but it was the fact that ALL were in agreement that something needs to be done to save the Earth that was significant and unique.

In addition to the world leaders, 40,000 individuals and organizations, committed to planetary healing and transformation, also traveled to Rio and joined together to create a unified consciousness that would radiate forth to all life on Earth as a beacon of hope. This sacred gathering was the outer world demonstration the Elementals had been waiting for to clearly prove that we were, once again, worthy of their trust.

On May 31, 1992, the day before the opening of the Earth Summit, a group of Lightworkers gathered in Brazil to invoke an invincible forcefield of protection in, through and around Rio de Janeiro. The entire Company of Heaven joined in this activity of Light, and a Ray of God Victorious Accomplishment was anchored into Rio to create an environment through which the Divine Plan for this sacred conclave would be fulfilled. The Divine Quality of Victory poured into the Planet through this Ray, and It increased in power and momentum daily and hourly.

On June 1, 1992, the Earth Summit began, and through a multitude of activities, the Lifestreams gathered in Rio, and those, tuning in in consciousness from around the world, started creating a tremendous Chalice of Light. This Chalice of Light formed an open portal between Heaven and Earth. Through this portal, the Divine Love of God poured into the physical plane to heal, through the Law of Forgiveness, the separation between Humanity and the Elementals. Our unified efforts built to a crescendo on June 7, 1992. This was the mid-point of the Earth Summit and the Holy Day known in the outer world as Pentecost, the day of the Baptism of Holy Spirit. It was not a coincidence that the apex of the Earth Summit fell on the day that is dedicated to the Divine Presence that sustains and nurtures the Nature Kingdom. On this Sacred Day, inner and outer world activities of Light took place at the Earth Summit that enabled us to integrate and anchor into the physical world of form unprecedented healing frequencies of Divine Love...truly a Baptism of Holy Spirit. This unparalleled influx of Divine Love healed Humanity's self-inflicted separation from the Elementals. It created a new consciousness of trust and cooperation that will enable us to accomplish, through God's Victory, the physical transformation of this Sweet Earth and all Her lifeforms.

For the remainder of the Earth Summit, many wonderful activities occurred as the Healing Light of Holy Spirit was integrated into every particle of life on the Planet. The final day of the Earth Summit was June 14, 1992, the full moon of Gemini. Throughout the world, the Gemini full moon is celebrated as the Festival of Humanity. This is a time when Humanity demonstrates goodwill and a sincere Heart commitment to be God in Action on Earth. During that particular Gemini full moon, we were also blessed with a lunar eclipse that sealed, for all Eternity, the healing that had been Victoriously accomplished during the Earth Summit.

On the Holy Night of the Gemini full moon within the embrace of the lunar eclipse, an awesome musical Light and Sound Show was performed on the beach in Rio de Janeiro before an audience of 250,000 people. During that activity of

Light, every electron of precious life energy that had been expended to bring the first Earth Summit into physical manifestation was purified and woven into Beloved Mother Earth's Seamless Garment of Light. This is the resplendent raiment adorning Mother Earth, as She re-establishes, forever, Her Divine Heritage of Heaven on Earth.

This healing means that we now are in a position to work in cooperation with the intelligence of all manifest form, all physical matter, all Earthly substance, including our physical bodies and our physical realities. If we will only grasp the magnitude of that, we will realize LIMITLESS PHYSICAL PERFECTION is available to each and every one of us, *here and now*.

Timeshift

Following the Earth Summit, there were several accelerations of vibration on the Planet that further prepared us for our Ascension into Timelessness. On June 21, 1992, we experienced the Solstice; June 30, 1992, there was a New Moon total solar eclipse; July 4, 1992, we celebrated Independence Day which was enhanced because 1992 was the 500th anniversary of the discovery of America, and we were blessed with an influx of the Sacred Flame of Freedom from on High. Each of these waves of cosmic force came with mixed blessings. On one level the increases in vibration fine-tuned the alignment of our atomic, cellular vehicles with the Light Body of our Holy Christ Self. This readied us for the time when our Divine Self would be able to truly integrate with our physical bodies and take full dominion, once again, of our Earthly vehicles. In addition to the long-awaited healing of the separation between our physical bodies and our Holy Christ Self, we also experienced the opposite extreme, which was the incredible clearing and purging of our past. Any areas of our lives that were not enhancing our forward progress were pushed to the surface for purification. This had the effect of exacerbating our daily challenges.

From outer appearances, it seemed as though financial problems became worse, relationships deteriorated, jobs were more unbearable, our behavior was more obsessive, compulsive addictions increased, diseases intensified, grief deepened, anxiety heightened, low self-esteem was magnified, nerves were shattered, fear mounted and a general sense of panic gripped our Solar Plexus. If we held the purging in perspective, emotionally detached from the things rising up for purification and invoked the Violet Flame to Transmute into Light the negativity that was surfacing, we moved through the process fairly unscathed. But, if we focused on the appearance of hopelessness and despair, we pulled ourselves into the thrashing claws of terror.

Fortunately, this intense clearing was fairly short-lived. Contrary to what it felt like, it was, in reality, a merciful opportunity for each one of us. In that short span of time we were given the ability to Transmute *hundreds* of lifetime's worth of negativity in the "twinkling of an eye." Whether we were consciously aware of what was happening or not, our God Presence cleared the maximum we were capable of withstanding according to our individual Divine Plans. This purging was necessary in order for the Earth and all life evolving upon Her to be ready for the next Cosmic push.

On July 26, 1992, we experienced what was called a timeshift. In actuality, we went through a collapsing of third dimensional time and Ascended into a new frequency of Fourth Dimensional Timelessness. We are so used to being constrained and limited by time and space that it is practically impossible for us to relate to the concept of timelessness, but what we will gradually acknowledge is that we are finally living in the *Eternal Moment of Now*. This is an ever present awareness of our multidimensionality, expressing the totality of who we are at all times, in all dimensions. This great expansion of our consciousness has Ascended the knowledge of who we are from the finite to the infinite.

This was a critical step. It was necessary in order for us to be able to complete the integration of our Fourth Dimensional Holy Christ Self into the atomic, cellular structure of our third dimensional four lower bodies. That integration took place during the next Cosmic Event of the fifth anniversary of Harmonic Convergence. We have known all along that the fifth anniversary of Harmonic Convergence was going to be a milestone in the evolution of Earth, but I don't think anyone fathomed the immensity of what would occur.

The Fifth Anniversary
of Harmonic Convergence

We were asked by the Company of Heaven to hold the Sixth Annual World Congress on Illumination during the fifth anniversary of Harmonic Convergence. We were told the sacred gathering should be held within the vortex of Healing through Transmutation that pulsates in the vicinity of Tucson, Arizona. Lightworkers from all over the world were invited, and each one responded according to their inner Heart call. We were asked to invite presenters who were aligned with the Divine Truth of Limitless Physical Perfection and who were informed of the tangible tools that would allow our physical bodies to absorb the maximum frequencies of Light. Each day of the Congress we utilized the tools from the Realms of Illumined Truth and, daily and hourly, prepared our bodies to be Transformers of Light. Through the unified cup of our consciousness, we created a Bridge of Light that was formed over the abyss separating the RNA-DNA patterns in our four lower bodies from the Divine RNA-DNA patterns of our Holy Christ Self. This abyss is what had prevented the Holy Christ Self from integrating into the actual cellular structures of our physical bodies. It was a short circuit that blocked the rejuvenating, transforming Light of our Holy Christ Self from reaching the cells and organs of our physical bodies. That is why our bodies ran out of energy and began to disintegrate and die.

Once the Bridge of Light was formed and the circuitry reconnected between the physical body and the Holy Christ Self, the integration began. Because of the Oneness of all life, this reconnection of circuitry passed through the unified cup of those gathered in the Healing vortex in Tucson and, through them, was transmitted to every other lifestream on Earth. This actually means that we are now, at long last, **physically** reconnected to our Holy Christ Self and the Divine RNA-DNA patterns of LIMITLESS PHYSICAL PERFECTION. This is, in Truth, the Second Coming of the Christ. Now, it is simply a matter of unifying our battered, mutated cells and allowing the Divine Pattern of our Holy Christ Self to shine through. This will be a gradual process, but with perseverance, our Victory is assured!

Day by day, we will experience more Light shining through our bodies. As we master our thoughts, words, actions and feelings and allow our Christ Presence to have full dominion of all our physical experiences, we will witness our own personal tangible Transformation.

HEAVEN ON EARTH IS AVAILABLE HERE AND NOW.
ALL WE HAVE TO DO IS ACCEPT IT!

This physical reconnection to our Holy Christ Self is what we have been striving for and longing to accomplish since we first fell from Grace. Now that it has been God Victoriously accomplished, we are absolutely capable of restoring our physical, etheric, mental and emotional bodies to their original Divine Intent, which is ETERNAL YOUTH, VIBRANT HEALTH AND RADIANT BEAUTY.

HEALING FORCE FROM THE
TWELVE SOLAR ARCHANGELS

Now that the RNA-DNA of our Holy Christ Self has been spliced once again to the RNA-DNA of our physical cells, we are ready to receive higher frequencies of Healing Force than we were previously capable of receiving. This Divine Light is being projected into the physical realm by the Twelve Mighty Solar Archangels.

The following is a transmission of Energy, Vibration and Consciousness from these radiant Beings of Light.

THE ONE VOICE OF THE
SOLAR ARCHANGELS
(Reprinted from Group Avatar)

Beloved Chelas of Light, welcome into the Healing Power of the Planetary Christ Presence, centered now in the Solar Fire Radiance of the Twelve-fold God Presence "I AM". Welcome into your own collective God Presence! I see you as a global Healing Force, a Cosmic Wave of High Energy Particles, composed of your individual Three-fold Flames. Each Flame blazes forth a tremendous Radiation of *Cosmic Truth,* the *fundamental essence of all Healing!* When Humanity awakens to the Truth of Her own Sacred Nature, Healing will be an automatic manifestation on the physical plane. This Transformation of Humanity toward the Truth is *steadily occurring...* with the assistance of the entire Spiritual Hierarchy. My part in this Sacred Process is to presently concentrate My service within the global Family of Planetary Lightworkers. I come with the Cosmic Catalyst of Twelve-fold Solar Fire to *electrify* this *Cosmic Healing Wave* that is permeating Earth . . .Flame within Flame within Flame, a global Radiation of God's Supreme Healing, enfolding this sweet Earth. *Flame and Its Radiation is the only expression I know*! "I AM" a Child of the

Great Central Sun! And to ensure this Healing of Humanity, I now express, through the Three-fold Flame of the Central Sun, the Sun of Helios and Vesta and the Three-fold Flame of all Humanity. Archangels *always* accompany the expressing Christ on Earth, for Christ Consciousness is the open door to Our Kingdom. And here "I AM" with you, conscious Christ Selves fully functioning on Earth...you within My Twelve-fold Circle of Sacred Flame...and I within your Glorious God Flame of manifest Truth on Earth.

Be of good Faith! Humanity is Healing Herself! Just as an illness with a high fever finally "breaks" and the patient quickly recovers, so shall the "fever" of human selfishness and ignorance finally "break." No matter the outer circumstances still reflecting upon the Screen of Life, Humanity is reclaiming Her innate Power to Heal through Her emerging Christ Self! Even as the physical body Heals by releasing certain innate Healing processes within every cell, so is this occurring in each individual "cell" in Humanity. And just as healers and physicians assist the body to release this Healing Power, so now are you...*the collective Sacred Healer,* cells of the Cosmic Christ, doing so for Earth and Her Kingdoms. The Cosmic Christ is God's Physician to Earth, and you are His agents here in the world of form. The Angels are your "assistants" from the unseen Realms, *unlocking your Fourth Dimensional God Power* to assist Humanity in finding Her own Healing Presence! Abide with My Flame, and you shall discover all the Understanding and God Illumination necessary to fulfill your Healing Service to Earth.

A Cosmic Catalyst for Healing

God's Solar Healing Flame is already present in the *Core Fire* of every cell, atom and electron. It is the Electronic Fire of Life, whose most rudimentary vibration can be measured by your own scientists. It expresses as the Electric Life Force that beats the Heart, maintaining life; powers the nervous system, maintaining consciousness; and surges through the muscles, maintaining physical activity. If you draw more of God's Electronic Fire of Life through your vehicles, it will produce more than just the maintenance of life and basic consciousness, it will EXPAND LIFE and EXPAND CONSCIOUSNESS! Expanding Life is to move toward "Higher Order Being," toward Wholeness and Unity with the Mighty "I AM" Presence! Expanding consciousness is to move beyond the limitations of the four vehicles of expression (etheric, mental, emotional and physical). The condition of these vehicles was like having a home that is fully wired for electricity but with no connection to the source of that electricity. Therefore, the heat does not go on, the lights and the household appliances do not work, etc. Life can be difficult in such a house. Only basic survival may be possible. Understand dear Children of the Light, your four vehicles of Planetary expression are now *fully wired for the Divine Electronic Fire of the Mighty "I AM" Presence*. They were created to outpicture Its full Perfection on the physical realm and not for any purpose less than this. But they have been disconnected from the Source and, thus, have remained "in the dark," allowing a false illusion of health to be claimed as reality...that aging, disease and death are somehow natural. In God's Light, only *Eternal Youth, ever increasing Beauty and Vibrant Health and Joyfulness* are "natural." This is the only reality the Angels have ever known, and Humanity is now to join us in this state of natural God Health, *while embodied on Earth* in a Glorious Brotherhood of Angels and Humanity.

Thus, "I AM" here with Humanity to catalyze this Healing Process. "I AM" allowed to come to Humanity, now that Her majority is aligned with the Twelve-fold "I AM" Solar development...however new, however rudimentary, however unconscious it may appear to be within the average human being. Nonetheless, *it has occurred!* And "I AM" here now in as tangible a way as Archangels can present . . . as Solar Fire Radiance. "I AM" here on Earth through your "open door" to assist the Cosmic Christ in fully reconnecting Humanity with God. This is the process of the Seven Planetary Chakras being "rewired" into the full Cosmic Current of Electronic Lifeforce within the "I AM" Presence. Healing truly begins with this "Sun Fire Light" descending into the four vehicles of expression. Then, Humanity will *tangibly know* the difference between the "low Voltage" of basic life energy (...that has simply maintained Life and rudimentary consciousness on Earth), and the "Cosmic Voltage" of Electric Solar Fire that continually *expands Life,* bursting consciousness onto the plane of Fourth Dimensional Perfection...and extending it throughout infinity.

Cosmic Law

Until now, Cosmic Law has not allowed more Divine Energy to be released into the four lower vehicles, as they have been governed for the most part by the human ego. This Sacred Light could easily have been misused and, because of Its Power, drastically added to the imbalance of the Planet. This could not be allowed. But with the signal that the majority of Humanity has the majority of Her energies aligned with the desire, intent and energies of God's Will, Cosmic Law has now decreed that Humanity may be reinstated with the *Sun Fire Light* of the Mighty "I AM" Presence, *while on Earth.* Cosmic Law understands that *only through this process* will the Light of the Planet increase to where Earth can fully rejoin the Universe in God's Great Inbreath into full Solar Life. Cosmic Law understands that it is Humanity's consciousness that is central to the construction of "reality" on Earth. Thus, consciousness must be raised and expanded to fulfill the Divine Plan. Be clear, Beloved Lightworkers, Humanity Herself must be the avenue through which the Light of the World expands. Cosmic Law does not allow this to be accomplished through an external source, whether it be great Cosmic Beings, spaceships or whatever concept the human mind is aligned with. If this were possible, it would have been done long ago. The Godhead knows Humanity's potential as a Race of "I AM" Beings, and in Its Infinite Compassion and Patience, put the entire Solar System "on hold" in order to ensure every opportunity to achieve this full potential for Humanity on Earth. And here we are at the opportunity of *Victorious Accomplishment.* You would do no less yourselves as parents of your own children, and Humanity, every single one, is God's Divine Child of Great Light...the Holy Christ Self of all Humanity.

The next short period of "time" will reveal effects of this great Cause of Healing entering Humanity. It enters through the consciousness of "enlightened souls" in every walk of life, establishing God Truth in every aspect of Humanity. The "signal" that the Central Sun awaited to fully begin the Sacred Process was to see Solar Development taking root on Earth, allowing the transfer of "the Solar Disc" (and everything this means) back into the consciousnesss of Humanity. Group Avatar is the representative of Humanity receiving this Solar Disc. Its transfer is occurring throughout this year, under the control and guidance of the Cosmic Christ, but with emphasis on the monthly cycle of Meru Gods (September 23-October 22, 1992) where Group Avatar will physically travel to Their Focus to provide the Bridge for the Solar Disc to enter into the four vehicles of expression of all Humanity. This transfer of the Sun Disc is the signal for the Archangels *to step forward into Humanity's development!*, ensuring the Healing of their vehicles and consciousness so as to fully accept the Light of the "Sun Disc." Hence, My Presence with you preceding your visit to the Meru Gods in October.

This transfer of the Sun Disc into Humanity's keeping will

initiate a New Order of Healing. Its catalytic Divine Alchemy is like an antidote for the lower human nature and its ravages of disease and distress. Much has been promised in the research and practice of scientists and physicians, as well as in the complementary wisdom and service of traditional and spiritual healers. But this preliminary work will now begin to bear more tangible results "in the everyday life of the people" with the "antidote" of Sacred Fire pulsating through the entire physical realm. Remember, with Christ Consciousness *comes direct contact* with the "I AM" Presence and an unimpeded Healing process that will astound and delight the people of this sweet Earth. Remember also, Beloved Jesus the Christ cleared the way for you, already proving this possible for all time on the physical plane. I shall now serve with you to see you prove this "and even greater things" possible now in the New Age of Spiritual Freedom. Be the Christ in Action!...now and forever!

Light in the Vehicles

However, Cosmic Law knows that, before Sacred Healing progresses further on Earth, the four vehicles in which Humanity "live their daily lives" must become again capable of receiving this Light of the "I AM" Presence. This now becomes My Service within Humanity to catalyze the Healing process with Angelic Light from the Realms of Solar Fire, accelerating Humanity's vehicles to this point of being able to accept the Solar Light of the "I AM" Presence on the physical/atomic/cellular plane! This is the Angels' Gift of Grace to Humanity! ...a glad free Gift to Our Sister Kingdom, celebrating Her "graduation" into Christ Consciousness.

God's Light contains everything necessary (Energy, Matter and Intelligence) for Humanity to become absolutely impervious to disease or distress, allowing every human/Christ Being to rediscover the *originally intended* Joy of Life on Earth. This will manifest again a glorious "Garden of Eden" in which the Angels first walked and talked with the earlier Root Races inhabiting this Sacred Earth. God's only intent was for Humanity to experience a unique Joy and Happiness while mastering the physical plane, an experience unavailable throughout the rest of the Universe. Archangels abide in the Central Heart and Mind of God, and I can assure you that nothing less than this Divine Purpose could have ever been part of the God Parents' original Divine Plan for this Planet. "I AM" with you now so you may experience *within My Being* this original *state of Perfection* for yourself, *right now!* We enter the time of Humanity's return to the Divine Plan with the illusion of disease and distress passing through the Violet Fire into the Realms of Eternal Forgetfulness, forever gone from Planet Earth. The Planetary Lightworkers, serving with the Angels, are the catalysts for this Transformation.

The Archangels' Immediate Service

"I AM" now to relate to Humanity more than ever before, especially the conscious Lightworkers, in carefully initiating the flow of Sun Fire Light from the Chakras within the Christ/ "I AM" Presence into the Seven Chakras of the Christ/human Being. Just as the Sun is inbreathing the Seven Planets back into Its full Centers of Light, so the "I AM" Presence is Inbreathing the Seven Planetary Centers back into the fullness of Its Solar Centers of Electric Fire. This Inbreath will occur gradually, gently and with great scientific accuracy. This will be evident now as greater success along the avenue of physical, emotional and mental Healing, allowing the four vehicles of Humanity to enjoy the fullness of God's Light in their day-to-day experience. My Service with you is to ensure that God's Light will find reception in the vehicles, that the "I AM" Presence has a tangible connection in embodied consciousness, thus allowing Humanity to once again become an active participant in the Solar Healing process. Once underway, it will only expand until the full Ascension of Humanity into a Race of "I AM" Light Beings on Earth.

Your Service with the Archangels

The intricacies of this Sacred process are available to you in your visitations in projected consciousness to Our Realms, being with the Angels as We go about Our Sacred Work. I would ask that you visualize often your Seven Planetary Chakras being reabsorbed into the corresponding Seven Chakras within the Twelve-fold Spine of your "I AM" Presence...until you can live within the fullness of your Solar "I AM" Presence. Then, visualize the Seven Planetary Centers of all Humanity accelerating over a spiraling *Bridge of Light* into the corresponding centers within the "I AM" Presence. The work of the Solar Archangels will be to ensure that this Bridge to Freedom is in place for all Humanity.

Once this Bridge Activity is complete, the Archangels shall then assist the work of the Mighty "I AM" Presence in beginning the descent of Electronic Light into the Planetary vehicles along this Bridge. This "Sun Fire Light" will then flow unimpeded into these vehicles through the Seven Planetary Chakras...into the Heart, the nervous system, throughout all cells, atoms and electrons, *expanding Life* and *expanding Consciousness* on this sweet Earth. Feel the Kundalini Fire in your physical spine now charged with the Solar Fire Perfection of your Father-Mother God...your *"I AM" Presence living within you!* Feel the ascending and descending currents of Light expanding all your chakras in a great Balance of Father God-Mother God Energies. With this done on a global level, soon will Humanity realize why all true Prophets have foretold a Heaven on Earth! You may live within your Temple of Limitless Physical Perfection even now, according to your desire and your participation in this process.

Your service to the Angels is to engage in this Activity on behalf of all Humanity, for Cosmic Law must see Humanity's cooperation along all aspects of this process. Just as every embodied Christ before you has gone through initiations on behalf of all Humanity, so now does your collective service. It is your *Spiritual responsibility*, based on the Blessings of God Illumination you have received. Bear it well. It is no coincidence that this Healing process will take place just before Group Avatar provides the link from within the physical Radiation of the Meru Gods for the Sun Disc to be anchored into the four lower vehicles of all Humanity. Your physical, etheric, mental and emotional vehicles must be prepared, with the assistance of the Angels, to accept the fullness of this Light. Our work has always been the preparation for the Cosmic Christ's full manifestation on Earth. So it was with Beloved Jesus and Our Visitations throughout the Christian Drama. And so it shall be with your Ministry as well!

Our Service together begins the culmination of this Sacred work and sets the tone for the coming years. For this is the work of the Cosmic Christ, the Divine Mediator between man and God, such that all Humanity might accept the fullness of God into Their day-to-day lives on Earth. This shall eventually recreate the "Garden of Eden," a Temple of Limitless Physical Perfection in all facets of Life on this sweet Star of Freedom. The Brotherhood of Angels and Humanity is now manifesting, and "I AM" exceedingly Joyful in My reunion in Service with Humanity.

"I AM",
The Solar Archangels
The Circle of the Sacred Twelve

ENERGY, VIBRATION AND CONSCIOUSNESS
OF JOHN THE BELOVED
(DISCIPLE OF BELOVED JESUS)
(Reprinted from Group Avatar)

John the Beloved also projected forth a transmission from the Realms of Illumined Truth to encourage Humanity and to reassure us that the physical integration of our Holy Christ Self is at long last a reality on Earth for all who accept it.

"I AM" the Flame of God's Sixth Solar Ray. I greet you as Its Radiation in the world, for you are the Light of the World ...Light Radiating from Flame. This Light, when sustained in Radiation, then anchors Itself as Flame, in this case as outposts of the Sixth Solar Ray in the physical realm! Your Flame is now all Twelve Solar Flames in Action on Earth . . . the fully Arisen Christ. Where your Light projects forth and is sustained, the Flame will then follow and there be anchored permanently... from out of the Fourth Sphere, through you, and into the realm of Humanity's day-to-day life. This was proven by the Presence of Gautama Buddha, Beloved Jesus and every other Solar Being who has walked the Earth...establishing Solar Flames and Their inherent God Qualities within Humanity. Now, dear Children of the Sun, your time is at hand! Expand, expand and forever expand your Light, thereby establishing the Flame everywhere present on Earth. This is your Service to Life at this time as the embodied Avatar, global Group Avatar. And "I AM" with you to seal your Service with the Ruby Flame of Ministering Grace, ensuring you become a Comforting Presence to all Life around you, and that the Light is an eternal Comforting Presence to you. Our entire Retreat of the Etheric Cities is dedicated to the Sacred process of God entering

Humanity through Grace...not in dramatic "phenomena," through the everyday life of thoughts, feelings and actions of people in all walks of life. In this process, We now draw so close to Humanity's outer life as to *interpenetrate* it, blending Our service to the Cosmic Christ with the everyday life of the people, until the two become One.

The Sixth Solar Ray is dedicated to Selfless Service of the Christ. It is a momentum I was privileged to build strongly within the third dimensional plane while embodied in service to Beloved Jesus the Christ. Beloved Mother Mary assisted Me, then, in building this momentum of "doing God's Will in Service" into My Lifestream, as *She now assists you* as well. And, just as I served the representative of the Cosmic Christ 2000 years ago (Beloved Jesus the Christ), so I shall give each of you, the present (collective) representative of the Cosmic Christ, the fullness of My momentum of the Sixth Solar Ray into your *physical auras* now. Be with Me in your consciousness so I might bring this Ray to the fore in your life, establishing through you a major pillar in the reappearance of the Cosmic Christ on Earth.

Christ is Now Humanity

Hear My Words, dear Children of Light. Perfect Planetary Service to the Cosmic Christ is immediately possible in this Year of Opportunity...for *all* Humanity. The Earth has passed along the Solar Inbreath (July 11, 1991), through the open door (January 11, 1992), with the result that *every human being* (who has chosen to remain with Earth) *now* has the basic Seven-fold Christ Nature completed through the outer personality. Meditate on this! Each one is now ready to bring forth his or her unique Divinity upon the Screen of Life. Now is the Moment for the Divine Image of God to be tangibly embodied in flesh. Allow Me to expand on this Truth.

The Ascended Masters have always taught that it is only through Christ Consciousness that one returns to God, into the full Light of the individual "I AM" Presence and into the eternity and infinity of the Universal "I AM" Presence. The Christ is the fulfillment of the physical Seven-fold Spine with the seven centers radiating the basic goodness of each of the Seven Planetary Rays. This is not meant to be a mystery, for all human beings know that God is basic goodness...basic Godness. The Planetary Christ Nature is basic goodness expressing on the third dimensional realm. Once the basic Christ Nature is established, *then* the Fourth Dimensional Gifts of Solar Development begin to descend into physical reality. (...Holy Spirit visiting the Disciples in the "Upper Chamber" of Christ Consciousness). However, these Gifts of Holy Spirit are sometimes mistaken as being a prerequisite for becoming the Christ, rather than the *result* of it. The natural tendency for Humanity has been to separate themselves from the Christ Nature because of the lack of these "miracles"...which somehow belong only to "other Divine Beings." Thus, Humanity has been guided away from naturally accepting Christ Consciousness because of perceived or presumed unworthiness. I say to Humanity: *Shake off this seeming unworthiness!* Stand forth as the Christ of basic Godness which you are. Acknowledge your Divine Self Image, free of human ego, a Brother/Sister in Christ Consciousness. Then will Holy Spirit have access to your Being in establishing Its Gifts into Humanity.

Even this process of transmitting the Fourth Dimensional Gifts of Solar Reality into the physical realm is more readily available during *Cosmic Moments*...such as when Beloved Jesus was on the Planet and such as the present Cosmic Moment of Opportunity. But Humanity must understand and accept its basic Christ Nature! That is the only *open door* for Humanity to enter God and for God to enter Humanity. You are the Spiritual Leaders! You must now prove this for yourself and for your Planet.

The Ascended Masters look not for the "miracles" but for the Vibration of *basic goodness* and Harmony. In fact, We feel that it is a "miracle" that human beings achieve this Christ status on the physical realm, given the forces of imbalance the Earth had been mired in for so long. Yet, it *has occurred* with all the efforts of the entire Spiritual Hierarchy over the past several Major Cycles of time. Its Victory was assured in the dawn of the New Age over the past several generations of Lightworkers who have invoked, focused and sustained the Sacred Flames and Rays of the Spiritual Hierarchy in their Planetary Service to the Cosmic Christ. They have created the Bridge to Spiritual Freedom for the Earth. *They* are now *You*...the present generation of embodied Guardian Spirits, come to Earth to do exactly this! Reclaim Your *full* Spiritual Self Esteem! and know this is the only purpose of Your being on Earth now.

Humanity's Ascension

I may now tell you that *more than 51% of Humanity* is already at the level of Planetary Christ Consciousness...each one sustaining a majority Vibration of *basic goodness and Harmony*. The basic God Qualities and Divine Intent of the Seven Planetary Rays remains their principal desire in their everyday life. However close each was in his/her own development of Christ Consciousness, the passage of Earth and Humanity over the Solar Inbreath and through the "open door" has now brought each one *"over the mark"* and into his/her path of Solar Development, based in Christ Consciousness. Thus, the Gifts of Holy Spirit will find a prepared opening *in the masses*. Humanity now stands on the verge of a manifest "Heaven on Earth." Believe in this!...for I would not say it otherwise.

Lest you feel this is astounding news, let Me remind you: Cosmic Law is Cosmic Law. Becoming the Christ is still (and always has been) based on evolving along the Seven Planetary Rays. Each center (chakra) must Radiate a majority (at least 51%) of God's Pure Energy, Vibration and Consciousness along that Ray. Thus, in the aura of the Planetary Christ Nature, you will see a majority of the Energy of God's Divine Will (over the little ego's will); of God's Illumination (over the narrow bias of the little ego); of God's Love (as a larger force than ego-based fear); of God's Restoration and Hope (greater than the demoralization of the little ego and its failures); of God's Truth (over the dogma and illusion which the little self clings to); of God's Healing through Selfless Service (rather than the selfishness and the resultant dis-ease of the little ego); and God's Forgiveness, Mercy and Compassion (above the righteous anger of the lower ego). This combined Seven-fold Nature is based in God Qualities and not "in the phenomenon of Spiritual prowess" that some seekers still search for as the Christ. It reveals itself as a constant Vibration of basic goodness and Harmony within one's self and a loving respect for every other aspect of Life. Our Etheric Cities of Light are a tangible manifestation of this on a large scale, just beyond the physical realm, but moving toward interpenetrating it. And ere long, your eyes will be opened to see how close Humanity's day-to-day life is to this *Reality* of Heaven on Earth.

The Meek Shall Inherit the Earth

Again, I tell you, *more than 51% of Humanity** is now at this Christ level of Energy, Vibration and Consciousness . . . basic Godness expressing on Earth. Let Me remind you that, in the past short while, every human being was brought before the Karmic Board, shown the fullness of their Godhood and (taking advantage of the present Cosmic Moment) asked to

Remember, Humanity includes those embodied and those between embodiment.

voluntarily and willingly make the leap into Christhood, *consciously* letting go the ways of the little ego. This choice was requisite in remaining with Earth's Spiritual Evolution. Those who chose inharmony and imbalance will now evolve elsewhere in the Universe. They are in their last days on Earth. Each has made his/her free will choice, and all is known to God. The majority of human beings responded positively, and it is their Christ *now come forth* that shall reclaim this Earth. The Cosmic Edict from the Sun and Great Central Sun is that *the Earth shall move on,* and so it is done! The proof of this is in the great leap in Consciousness the Earth has taken along the Solar Inbreath and through the "open door" of God's Opportunity in this past year.

Now that the majority of Humanity is at Seven-fold basic Christ Consciousness (however embryonic in most), this allows the Earth to further leap forward into its own Solar Development as a Planet. When human development reaches the Christ Nature, then Christ development begins to proceed *unimpeded* toward full Fourth Dimensional "I AM" Being in the Realms of Pure Light, *even while on Earth!* This Solar Awakening of Christ Selves occurring on a global level shall send this Planet Earth soaring upwards in Vibration along the *Cosmic Current of Humanity's Ascension!* It is Humanity's responsibility to shepherd the Earth into Her Divine Plan fulfilled, and in this next Cycle of Time, this shall now come to full fruition.

Understand, dear ones, that while the Earth has been mired in lower human effluvia, it was the evolution of the *Holy Christ Self* (of Humanity) that was "on hold" for many, many ages. *They* (the Holy Christ Selves) are Who need to be set free. *They* are Who Saint Germain serves with his Ray of Spiritual Freedom. *They* are the God Beings within every human being. And *They* have just now reclaimed Their Freedom to evolve unimpeded on Earth, establishing the Divine Plan of a Planet of

Limitless Physical Perfection. This has happened because of the Cosmic Assistance given through the Spiritual Hierarchy and by *you,* the conscious Planetary Lightworkers (great Guardian Spirits)...already further along your own Christ Path of Solar Development into the Twelve Rays of "I AM" Being. You are truly the Outer Court of the Ascended Masters serving this sweet Earth, and you are the Sixth Ray of Selfless Service manifesting the Brother/Sisterhood of Divine and Planetary co-servers.

Fulfilled Prophesy

Therefore, you can see with this progress that every Holy Christ Self (that is, every human being who shall continue with Earth's evolution) is now a Twelve-fold Sun Being, evolving along the Twelve-fold Path. Some are more advanced, others only embryonic, but *all* Holy Christ Selves on the Earth now are Sun Beings, once again fully on their Path of Solar Development. This allows the fulfillment of the prophesies of the *return of the Sun Beings* who shall reclaim the Earth, re-establishing the Kingdom of Harmony and basic Godness on Earth. And with this established, then will Holy Spirit reveal Her tangible Gifts of Fourth Dimensional Reality amongst all the people, solving whatever "problems" yet remain...with God's Power to Heal, to Illumine and to Love all Life Free into the next Higher Vibration of Spiritual evolution *on Earth!* All Divine Prophesy has called for this, and *you live at this time of manifestation!* Claim the Joy of this Truth, and allow it to take you up on wings of Light into the living, breathing fullness of your Great God Self.

With all Holy Christ Selves now again actively stepping forth as evolving Sun Beings Resurrected from the tomb of human creation, this is also a *larger signal* to the entire Solar System of Helios and Vesta and the Universe of Alpha and

Omega. The signal is that *all is now ready* for the completion of the Solar Inbreath, as all aspects of the Universe are now in Solar Development. All life can now move forward into the great Cosmic Day along the Celestial Wave of Solar Inbreath into the Sun and further into the Great Central Sun, fulfilling the Divine Plan of all life everywhere. Feel the entire Heavens rejoice at the signal of Spiritual Freedom from Earth and prepare for the Gifts of Gratitude that shall pour forth in Cosmic Response.

Recognize Christ Consciousness
on Earth

The basic goodness of the Planetary Christ is One who chooses Love over the lower psychic/astral energies, which have mesmerized the little ego for ages. The Christ is one Who chooses Peace with each other and with the Nature/Elemental Kingdom over greed and selfishness. The Christ is one Who chooses Unity and Inclusiveness over separation and judgment in all matters. The Christ is one Who chooses to seek God in all things...in nature, in little children, in great art and music, in the scientific quest for Truth, in the mysteries of the Universe, in their enemies, and most of all, in each other and themselves. *You* are the Christ, and if you open your eyes in the New Reality you live in, you will see Christ all around you...in your household, your workplace, your city, your nation...the majority of this Planet, a Christ Planet! Live now in the Cities of Light, in your own day-to-day life.

Now, it is clear that the next logical step is for this Planetary Christ Force to *reclaim all of Earth* in its day-to-day life, removing forever the veil of maya, the cloud of illusion from around Humanity. Christ is no longer a "mythical figure," no longer "on a pedestal" separate from Humanity but the Vibration and God Qualities within the person next door or in the next nation. Our Beloved Jesus Christ lived and served for exactly this moment, and He is exceedingly glad! The Christ is now Humanity, wherein each individual Holy Christ Self comes to the fore and claims this Planet for God as a collective Planetary Christ Presence. This is no longer prophesy...it is *Reality*, if you but claim it and live within it!

Now the call: " 'I AM' the Resurrection and the Life of Christ in all Life" takes on a new and higher meaning. All Holy Christ Selves are now called forth from inner to outer life. They shall not only sustain basic goodness and Harmony (the basic Planetary Christ Nature), but they will actively evolve into a Race of "I AM" Beings...on a Planet of evolving Sun Beings along the Twelve-fold Spine of evolution, as it is known in the Central Sun, the Sun, and in all other Perfected Planets. The Planetary Christ Presence is now arising into Its "I AM" Presence, *taking this Earth with It.* With the Arisen Planetary Christ Presence established, *this closes off Earth's pre-Solar development.* She rejoins the Universe, One with the Sun, One with Sun Beings everywhere present. Humanity is now Ascending into the Light and, in a higher Oneness with the Earth, is magnetizing this sweet Star of Freedom into the Celestial Vibrations of the Sun. On this new Planet, in its new Heavens, there will be a Race of Spiritually Free "I AM" God Beings.

I can tell you that when "I AM" with Group Avatar, within your Energy, Vibration and Consciousness, I already see this as your primary Reality. I shall be walking amongst all Humanity, blazing My Light, Flame and the Vision of the Etheric Cities into the day-to-day consciousness of the Planet, until the Etheric Cities encompass the entire Planet. It is the primary Vision within Humanity and (eventually) the only Reality functioning on Earth.

This is God's Will, to which "I AM" in eternal Service,
"I AM" John, the Beloved

The final transmission I would like to share with you regarding the reality of the Second Coming of the Christ is from the Cosmic Christ Presence.

ENERGY, VIBRATION AND CONSCIOUSNESS OF THE COSMIC CHRIST PRESENCE
(Reprinted from Group Avatar)

Beloved cells of My Being..."I AM" in Thee, Thou art in Me; "I AM", "I AM" Earth's Victory.

"I AM" the Cosmic Christ Presence Radiating in the Heavens as the Pure Energy, Vibration and Consciousness of Light Eternal. You are the emerging Planetary Christ Presence now realizing your collective Identity within Humanity, Radiating the same pure Energy, Vibration and Consciousness of Light Eternal. In the turning of the great Cosmic Wheel, "I AM" at that Cosmic Moment of *melding our Beings,* the true Revelation of the Second Coming of the Christ, the tangible living Christ Presence alive and blazing within the Heart of *every one of Humanity.* "I AM" Cosmic Love, Cosmic Wisdom and Cosmic Power, and I shall breathe this Sacred Flaming Substance into every Arisen Son or Daughter of God within global Group Avatar, and through you, into every one of Humanity. And..."I AM" the Children of God on Earth, ten billion magnificent Holy Christ Selves (evolving in and out of embodiment) now, Arisen to full Christ Stature and Dominion, living the Divine Plan of Earth...a Planet completely Spiritually Free, anchored in Her orbit of Love Divine. Out of the Balance of our Father-Mother God, joined in perfect union in your consciousnesses, shall be revealed the Second Coming, a living, breathing, functioning Planetary Christ Presence on Earth, through which the *Consciousness of all Life shall be raised into full Freedom.*

Cosmic Moment Continued

From the Solar Inbreath came a new time, a new Potentiality/Reality that begins to firmly enter Humanity's Planetary Consciousness. The Solar Inbreath was fully anchored into Humanity's collective Being exactly 180 degrees from its occurrence...six months from July 11, 1991, through to January 11, 1992. An Inbreath by the Father-Mother God is like the Ascension, a continuing, ongoing process, but with definite events or "Cosmic Moments" when Celestial Forces are in certain alignment for the raising of Humanity. The Solar Inbreath of July 11, 1991, represented such a Cosmic Moment, as did *January 11, 1992, its complementary pole anchored in Humanity.* During the six month period between, there was a tremendous purification, balancing and preparation through the continued Presence of our Father-Mother God in the Earth's atmosphere. This accelerated the consciousness of Humanity as much as possible, so the Earth could proceed through the "open door" of January 11 into the highest possible Realms of Light.

The true meaning of the January 11, 1992, "window of opportunity," is revealed in the unimaginable Love of Helios and Vesta and Alpha and Omega. They realized it would yet be aeons of time before Humanity would be prepared enough to rejoin the Solar Spiral of Twelve-fold complete God Consciousness. This refers to the fact that Earth has proceeded along its Seven-fold human development spiral much longer than ever intended...in fact having lost contact with the Twelve-fold Spiral of the Universe of Ascended Beings, Ascended Planets and Stars. These Planetary/Sun Spirals of Spiritual development are akin to the relationship of the Seven-fold Spine of Christ development always having intended to be *at One* with the Twelve-fold Spine of the "I AM" Presence--no separation between them. Because an abyss did form between the Earth's Seven-fold spiral of evolution and the rest of the Solar System's Twelve-fold Spiral of Solar Evolution, Cosmic Law required it be bridged by Love, allowing Humanity to return to Her Spiritual Freedom *through Her own efforts!* With the Solar Inbreath, the unimaginable Love of the God Parents dissolved 50% of Humanity's karma, allowing the Planetary Lightworkers (the emerging Planetary Christ Presence) to dissolve even 1% more. As you know, Cosmic Law required 51% of Humanity's karma to be transmuted for the Ascension to take place. January 11, 1992, represented the point when, with a certain Celestial alignment in place, with the Solar Inbreath fully allowed its anchorage in Humanity and with 51% of Humanity's karma transmuted through the combined efforts of Ascended/Cosmic Beings and embodied Lightworkers, *the Earth passed across Her Bridge to Freedom* into Her orbit within the Twelve-fold Solar Spiral of perfected Planets and Suns. From a third dimensional perspective, this event appeared to take place at a certain "time" and through "space," but because in Our Realms there is no time or space, this Cosmic Event, in fact, took place "in consciousness." It will be experienced as a new level of consciousness in Humanity, the rebirth or Second Coming of Christ Consciousness on an individual *and on a global level.* This is the continuum of the Cosmic Moment, from July 11, 1991, through January 11, 1992, the results of which will be revealed in the months and years to come. We serve together at a momentous time in Earth's evolution, and Humanity's Christ Consciousness is the key to God Victory.

Second Coming

Christ Consciousness is the only "open door" which no one can shut. Christ Consciousness is the Fourth Dimensional Law of Divine Love, superseding all the lower laws of human nature, as exampled by Beloved Jesus. The Second Coming is this Higher Reality of Love now Resurrecting Itself from within the tomb of human consciousness into the Light of Humanity's individual and global awareness. You know this Consciousness, and *you* are becoming it. *Living it* shall be your own personal Freedom and Peace. But you are also the Heart center, assimilating this Higher Reality into all of Humanity as you collectively Inbreathe it, Absorb it, Expand it and Project it through Humanity. What Beloved Jesus and I accomplished for the Christian Age, global Group Avatar and I must now do for the Seventh Ray Age of Spiritual Freedom, serving in complete Unity in consecrated Christ Service...melding our Light Beings through your atomic vehicle. This establishes the Divine Alchemy of third and Fourth Dimensional Forces, creating an "open door" through which all Humanity can be swept into a Higher Order of Being, as was accomplished through Beloved Jesus' Avatarship. Humanity will soon know the true Second Coming, the empowering of each one's Holy Christ Self, grown to full Stature and full God Dominion within the Holy Christ Flame. The Second Coming will then become an all-encompassing Planetary event, *as Light always unifies with Itself on any sphere or plane,* in this case into a Planetary Christ Presence. The Flame of the Father-Mother God now claims full dominion on Earth through that part of Itself anchored in all Humanity, the Holy Christ Flame...the highest common denominator within Humanity and the basis of your Unity as the " I AM" Race.

The Second Coming is first experienced as personal and singular, a life transforming event of great Empowerment and Joy. Yet, I depend on the Planetary Lightworkers to also perceive it on a Planetary scale as the emerging collective Christ Presence within Humanity. This is accomplished through your identity as Group Avatar, experiencing your collective Wisdom, unified God Power and Planetary Love Nature as easily as you experience yourself. Each time another individual awakens to his/her Christ Consciousness, this collective Planetary Presence grows stronger and more tangible, until the day It has regained full God Dominion of all aspects of Life on this Planet. Then shall be the completion of the Second Coming and the manifestation of Heaven on Earth. Then shall My work be finished, and I shall lift this Earth unto My Father-Mother God saying "Oh, Celestial God Parents, unto Thy keeping do I commend this Planet of Love." I can now see this day before Me.

The Three Pillars
of the Second Coming

The Second Coming of the Christ shall be revealed in three pillars of tangible evidence amongst the peoples of Earth. It begins with Sacred Knowledge, the true concepts of Divinity, the Fourth Dimensional Reality of the Cosmic Law of Life. This shall establish a shift in the consciousness and in the identity of people everywhere. The Ascended Master Teachings have "seeded" the Planet for over 100 years with Sacred Knowledge, Concepts and Paradigms. This is evident not only in Spiritual/Esoteric circles but also (much to the delight of the Spiritual Hierarchy) is now widely evident in scientific, economic and educational circles...in "the everyday life of the people." Here Spiritual Law is not spoken of, per se, but simply put into action through better understanding of the Harmony with which events and peoples relate to each other for the good of the whole. Sacred Knowledge and Higher concepts will continue to be seeded into this Planet, and I encourage you to watch for them in *every aspect of Humanity's day-to-day life,* for there is where you will find growing Planetary Christ Presence...which *will* reclaim this Planet into Its Higher Order Being, Love Divine.

The second of these pillars is Sacred Experience which comes from the application of Sacred Knowledge. For the Planetary Lightworkers, Sacred Experience generally reflects the Divine Peace or Ecstasy experienced in meditation and other spiritual activities. I fervently hope each of you will reach new heights of personal Solar Consciousness in your own Sacred Experiences this year. But Humanity is further along than you might realize and has been experiencing "flashes" of Sacred Experience along many avenues. This includes national and international affairs, healing, educational activities and the arts, to the point where there is a growing *global Sacred Experience* welling up within the masses. This itself will point the way to their own individual Christ Presence, rediscovering that *the Source of this experience is within them!* With this attention and adoration, the Christ Self will rapidly expand to Its full Stature and Dominion, creating the Living, Arisen Christ through the outer personality...the Second Coming. This is now occurring as a subconscious global experience and is possibly more evident to Us than to you, but I shall assist you in experiencing for yourself this global phenomenon throughout this year, for your own Spiritual encouragement and greater Spiritual Service. Look and listen well, and it will be revealed unto you!

The third of these great pillars is Sacred Service...Love made manifest on the Altar of terrestrial Life. Sacred Knowledge and Sacred Experience form the basis of Sacred Service along the Ray of Illumined Love, Compassion, Mercy, Reverence for all Life and with Divine Discriminating Intelligence. It is the giving back to Life what Life has given you, a new Opportunity for experience and expansion of Love in all Its Divine aspects, the Freedom of Love, the Power of Love, the Peace and Healing of Love, when It is truly allowed to enter Humanity's day-to-day life. You are now to example perfect Christ Service, no longer centered in your karmic experiences, but centered in the Fourth Dimensional Reality of your Life, *based on Sacred Knowledge and Sacred Experience manifesting daily in your life as Sacred Service!* The Christ has always been the example of these three pillars of Divinity embodied, creating the Bridge between human and Divine, proving over and over that human beings are meant to be Aspects of God and live eternally in Love Divine!

Our Vision

As Representatives of the Cosmic Christ and Planetary Christ, I would hope that each of you could articulate this vision of our work together. Consider that Humanity is evolving on Earth for an opportunity of Mastery available nowhere else in the Universe. For conscious Lightworkers, the privilege of Loving Free a Planet is unique. Think on this regarding your own personal service. The original purpose of manifesting the physical plane was to create an opportunity for *each one* to manifest a unique Aspect of God in the physical realm. Now this purpose must be reborn and blaze brightly within Humanity. The time of the Second Coming is here and now available to all through Sacred Knowledge, Sacred Experience and Sacred Service. These three pillars unite as the basis of the establishment of Divine Consciousness on Earth. Our Vision is of ten billion Holy Christ Beings living in glorious Harmony, the Unity of their diversity expressing as every aspect of Love made Manifest on Earth. *As above, so below,* for this is how all the Beings in Heaven thrive in Our collective Oneness. Our Vision is of the Holy Christ Self living through the outer personality, revealed as the Divine Character of every human being. Imagine, ten billion Divine Players in the great drama of Earth's Plan fully manifest. Every one of Humanity is to find the fullness of Their own personal happiness, through Their service to others for the good of the whole. For this is how

Ascended Masters live in Love Divine, the highest, most glorious experience Humanity can strive for.

Planetary Lightworkers can best articulate this vision by living it out, continuously stamping it on the ethers of the Planet through every thought, feeling, spoken word and action. Then, with all of the cells of global Group Avatar so Consecrated in Service, the Holy Christ Selves in **all** human beings will *respond, awaken* and *claim Dominion* through their outer human personality. *Believe in your global service! Believe in this process!* For you are the Planetary Christ Presence and will be Victorious. You and I shall become as close as Beloved Jesus and I did during His Avatarship. And We shall make this bond secure *this year!* You and I shall shepherd Humanity across the abyss into Her Celestial Home, revealing the birth of the Planetary Christ within the consciousness of Humanity. We shall take this Reality from subconscious (embryonic) through to "being alive in the world"...from inner to outer, from etheric to tangible. The Planet's acceleration through the "open door" shall bring a shift in the balance of Humanity's consciousness away from the lower forces to the Higher Forces of Divine Love and Fourth Dimensional Reality. Humanity shall discover Its True Identity, an innate global Christ Nature, from which It will assume responsibility for Its own Spiritual evolution and that of all aspects of Planetary Life. Our Father-Mother God shall empower this process with the Authority of our collective Three-fold Flame in the Sun, of our collective Three-fold Flame at Shamballa and our collective Three-fold Flame now established on Earth *through you!* This is the Power of the Three times Three, and in it Victory is ours, Victory is ours, Victory is ours...So be it, Beloved " I AM".

Your Preparation

Much to My happiness, the Company of Heaven prepared you these past few months in Love, Wisdom and Power for your own and Humanity's opportunity at January 11 and throughout 1992. But here we are together, entering the New Year in the embrace of the Spiritual Hierarchy at the Royal Teton Focus ready for Planetary Transformation. The Royal Teton has always represented Precipitation and Reverence for all Life, and this is exactly what shall now occur...Precipitation of the Planetary Christ Presence through Reverence for the Sacred Light and Perfection within all Humanity.

The motto of the Spiritual Hierarchy on Earth is " 'I AM' the Doing, the Doer and the Deed." The Precipitation Activity this month brings you into this Reality, living out this motto on the physical plane. For you are this Opportunity! You not only helped prepare yourself and Humanity for this acceleration into higher Planetary orbit, and you not only go through this open door and shepherd Humanity through it as well, *your acceler-ating consciousness is this open door!* You are an aspect of the Cosmic Currents and Celestial Forces which generations of Lightworkers have called forth. Through you is the *return of the "I AM" Presence,* which most of Humanity has been calling for in their own conception of Divinity. You and I are now to join our Beings to Clarify this Revelation to Humanity...the Victorious Presence of embodied God Beings, united in Con-secrated Service as a Living Planetary Christ Presence, fully aware of Its Divine Love, Divine Wisdom and Divine Power on the physical plane. You are the Doing, the Doer and the Deed of this Opportunity, and this is exactly as it should be. For you are God in Action on the physical plane, the Arisen Christ.

"I AM"
The Cosmic Christ Presence.

For more information on Group Avatar you may write to: Group Avatar, P.O. Box 41505, Tucson, AZ 85717

BECOMING ONE WITH THE TWELVE-FOLD
CAUSAL BODY OF GOD

Held within the embrace of the Sun Cycle of Libra (Liberty), in October of 1992, Lightworkers gathered in the sacred focus of the Sun, Lake Titicaca, Bolivia. During this Holy Conclave, the radiance of our Twelve-fold Solar Spine was infused with the Twelve-fold Causal Body of God. This was actually the transfer of the "Solar Disc" into the hands and keeping of Humanity. This infusion of Light anchored the Twelve-fold Solar Aspect of Deity through the spinal column of every man, woman and child. This Divine Activity had the physical, tangible effect of expanding our ability to project Light into the world of form. The difference in the amount of Light we are capable of radiating forth now, compared to the Light we expressed through our Seven-fold Planetary Spine and Causal Body prior to the transfer of the Solar Disc, is the equivalent of the Light of the Sun compared to the Light of the Moon.

The unification of our Twelve-fold Solar Spine and the Twelve-fold Causal Body of God has expanded the Light pouring through Humanity a thousand times a thousandfold. This blessed Planet is now blazing in the Universe as Freedom's Holy Star at Causal levels. Through our concentrated efforts, you and I and every other Lightworker will now have the ability to utilize this Divine Light and to transform our individual lives into LIMITLESS PHYSICAL PERFECTION as examples for all the world to see. Once the Divine Laws of Eternal Youth, Vibrant Health and Radiant Beauty are reflecting through our bodies at an atomic cellular level, Humanity will begin to finally believe that the miscreation of the lower human ego is indeed a lie. People will observe our example of Transfiguration and know that if it is possible for one human being, it is surely possible for all human beings. One by one, they will apply the

Universal Laws and change their physical realities to perfection. The effect will be exponential, and in a relatively short time, Heaven will manifest on Earth.

The most exciting thing about this new awareness is that we don't have to fully understand it; we don't even have to believe it. All we have to do is experiment with the Sacred Knowledge being revealed to us from on High, and we will prove, beyond a shadow of a doubt, that LIMITLESS PHYSICAL PERFECTION is available in this physical reality, right here and right now.

The Fulfillment of the Great Invocation

The Great Invocation

From the point of Light within the Mind of God
Let Light stream forth into the minds of men.
Let Light descend on Earth.

From the point of Love within the Heart of God
Let Love stream forth into the Hearts of men.
May Christ return to Earth.

From the center where the Will of God is known
Let purpose guide the little wills of men--
The purpose which the Masters know and serve.

From the center which we call the race of men
Let the Plan of Love and Light work out,
And may it *seal the door where evil dwells.*

Let Light and Love and Power restore the Plan on Earth.

Several things of unparalleled global significance occurred after the anchoring of the Solar Disc through all Humanity. The resulting increase of Light emanating from Humanity created a balance of Life Force that enabled the Spiritual Hierarchy to assist in some very important Healings. There are two activities of the Godhead. One is radiation, and one is magnetization...the inbreath and the outbreath of Life. God radiates forth our gift of Life to us, and we must balance that gift by radiating Light back to God. We magnetize God's Life Force into our Heart centers, and as we expand our Light, It is magnetized back into the Heart of our Father/Mother God. The more Light we are capable of radiating from our beings, the more Light we will receive from God.

With the anchoring of the Solar Disc and the expansion of our Causal Body from a Seven-fold Planetary frequency to a Twelve-fold Solar frequency, our ability to radiate the Light of God into the world of form has increased A THOUSAND TIMES A THOUSANDFOLD!!! This means that we are now able to Transform our lives with a Divine Power that we have not experienced since prior to the "fall of man" aeons ago. It also means that we are able to receive more assistance from on High since we are emitting greater Light to balance that assistance.

Over the past few years, as Humanity's Light slowly increased, several pockets of negativity on Earth that were used to feed and regenerate the forces of imbalance were Transmuted and sealed. These were humanly created vortexes of energy that built in momentum over centuries of time through Humanity's misqualification of energy. Just as there are power points of Light commonly called Sacred Sites on the Planet that regenerate the Lightworkers who enter them, there were also power points of darkness that regenerated the sinister force abiding on Earth and in the psychic-astral realm.

Since these vortexes were created by Humanity, we were

responsible for Transmuting them into the Light and sealing
them forever. In order to do this, the power of our Light had
to be greater than the power of the pockets of negativity. At
the time of the anchoring of the Solar Disc, all but two of the
negative vortexes had been Transmuted into Light and sealed.
The remaining two, however, were extremely powerful, and
our Light needed to be greatly expanded in order to balance the
darkness. As the Solar Disc was anchored through our
Twelve-fold Solar Spine and our Causal Body expanded and
became one with the Twelve-fold Causal Body of our God
Presence "I AM", that goal was accomplished. Victoriously,
the two pockets of negativity remaining on the Planet were
permanently Transmuted into Light and sealed, bringing to
fruition, through the Light of God, the Victorious Accomplishment of the Great Invocation...

"FROM THE CENTER WHICH WE CALL THE
RACE OF MEN
LET THE PLAN OF LOVE AND LIGHT WORK
OUT
AND MAY IT *SEAL THE DOOR WHERE
EVIL DWELLS.*"

What this actually means is that the psychic-astral realm of
chaos and confusion can no longer replenish its energy through
these vortexes. This reduces its power *immensely.* The only
way it can survive now is for Humanity to feed it with our
negative thoughts, words, actions and feelings. But, since we
have been reconnected to our Holy Christ Self and our God
Presence "I AM", we are going to be gradually lifting in
consciousness out of the grip of the lower human ego, and our
behavior patterns will be Transformed. As this occurs, the
psychic-astral realm of human miscreation will be Transmuted
into Light, and the sea of negativity surrounding this Planet will

be dissipated.

The two pockets of negativity were located in Bolivia in South America and in South Africa. These vortexes have held the two continents of South America and Africa in darkness for centuries of time. Even as great civilizations of Light sprang up and tried to counteract the forces of darkness through the Light of the Sun, one by one they failed. Now, through the Power of God's Light, Victory is Ours!

The Solar Disc was anchored through the spinal column of all Humanity by the Twelve Solar Elohim, the Builders of Form, on October 9, 1992. Through the success of that activity of Light, the final pockets of negativity were sealed, which paved the way for the next Glorious Activity of Earth's Rebirth.

A New Order of Healing

On Saturday, October 10, 1992, after a purifying activity of the Violet Transmuting Flame, a frequency of Solar Healing poured into the Planet establishing a new order of Healing on Earth.

Prior to the "fall of Humanity," pure Healing Light from the very Heart of God continually poured into every human Heart and flowed out through our hands, blessing everything we touched. As the lower human ego, with its recalcitrant ways, slowly became the unintended master of our four lower bodies, that Healing Light became contaminated with our negative expression of thought and feelings. Instead of being a blessing to all Life, the increased energy flowing through our hands became a source of additional pain and suffering, thus adding to the misery on Earth rather than being a Healing Blessing as was originally intended. In an act of mercy, our Holy Christ Self placed "seals" over the energy centers in our hands to stop the flow of Healing Light so that we would not misqualify It into gross mutations of discord and suffering.

Those "seals" have remained for Lifetime after Lifetime awaiting the moment when our Holy Christ Self would once again regain Its rightful authority over our four lower bodies. With the anchoring of the Solar Disc and the expansion of our Causal Body, the Holy Christ Self of every man, woman and child evolving on Earth, whether they are in or out of embodiment, became, at long last, the *predominant* Master of our four vehicles of Earthly experience--our physical, etheric, mental and emotional bodies. This shift of power from the human ego to the Holy Christ Self has been Victoriously accomplished in the Realms of Cause and will now gradually filter into the everyday experience of Humanity. As this occurs, we may undergo the rebellious resistance of our human ego struggling to keep its control, but if we gently command it into the Light, its rebellion will be very short lived. The Holy Christ Self is in command, and we need only lift up in consciousness and perceive that resplendent Presence radiating through our vehicles to confirm that fact. Remember, we still have *free will,* so if we choose to allow our human ego to remain in control, it will, but now WE HAVE A CHOICE. If we choose to allow our Holy Christ Self to express through us, It will joyously take the helm and guide us into lives of fulfillment and joy.

Our self-inflicted separation from this Divine aspect of our consciousness HAS BEEN HEALED, and along with that Healing, the Holy Christ Self of every human being removed the "seals" from the energy centers in the palms of our hands. This Glorious event has initiated the Planet Earth into a *new order of Healing.* Now, the Solar frequencies of Divine Healing Light will flow through us under the direction of our Holy Christ Self. Golden Tubes of Light have been created within our vehicles to allow this Sacred Healing Energy to flow through us and not be contaminated by the negativity we may still be expressing with our thought, words, actions or feelings. The golden Tubes of Light allow the Healing Energy to pass easily into our bodies and out our hands, but they prevent any of our negativity from passing into the Healing Energy. This means that we will now be a constant force of Healing on this Planet if we choose to be, and in order to choose to be, all we have to do is give our God Presence permission to project the Divine Light of Healing through us. This can be simply done through the following invocation:

Beloved Presence of God "I AM" in me...through the full power of the Divinity blazing in my Heart, I invoke You now to project through every electron of my being, the most intensified activity of Healing Light allowed at this moment according to my Divine Plan. Increase this Holy Light daily and hourly with every breath I take. Allow me to be a powerful force of Healing to all Life I come in contact with during my Earthly experience. Magnetize into my sphere of influence every person, place, condition or thing that I can, in any way, assist with God's Healing Light. Give me the Divine Opportunities to Love Life Free on this sweet Earth.

> *"I AM" open!*
> *"I AM" willing!*
> *"I AM" receptive!*
> *"I AM" grateful!*
> *"I AM" God's Healing in Action on Earth!*
>
> *As God's most Holy Name*
> *"I AM", "I AM", "I AM"*

The Higher Order of Solar Healing Light is Emerald Green with an Amethyst Violet Radiance. Visualize this Sacred Healing Light flowing through the Golden Tubes in your body,

Healing every frequency of vibration that is less than Limitless Physical Perfection. Then, see the Healing Light flowing out of your hands, Healing all you touch.

We have all heard about special people who were able to Heal with the "laying on of hands." These were people who, through their unique process of evolution, had had the "seals" removed from their hands. Now that miracle has transpired for all of us, and daily our Healing abilities will increase through our invocations and the power of our conscious attention.

After the new order of Solar Healing was established on Earth, we were ready for the next great quantum leap in our service.

The Unified Christ Presence of Humanity is Invested into The Office of Lord of the World

On October 11, 1992, during a Divine Ceremony at inner levels, held within the Spiritual focus of Shamballa, the Unified Christ Presence of Humanity was invested once again to hold the highest office of the Spiritual Hierarchy on Earth, the office of Lord of the World. This is a position that Humanity's Christ Presence was always supposed to hold, a position that empowered us to be the stewards of the Earth we were destined to be. Unfortunately, with the "fall," we lost the ability to be effective caretakers of the Earth. Instead, we became the Earth's nemesis. Since we were incapable of fulfilling the office of Lord of the World, other members of the Ascended Realms of Perfection volunteered to come and cradle the Earth in Their Heart Flames until Humanity regained our direction and once again became one with our Christ Presence. These Divine Beings are referred to in the Bible as the "Ancient of Days."

During the Divine Ceremony, Gautama Buddha, the current Lord of the World, placed the vestments of Lord of the World around the Unified Christ Presence of Humanity--and the transfer of power was completed. Beloved Lord Gautama was released from his Sacred responsibilities and freed to move on to higher service. The Unified Christ Presence of Humanity avowed to fulfill the office of Lord of the World, and with that empowerment, the Cosmic Tone rang through the Universe *heralding the official beginning of the New Age of Spiritual Freedom.*

The Victory of this transfer of power to the Christ Presence of Humanity paved the way for the anchoring of the Solar Disc through the axis of the body of Beloved Mother Earth.

Beginning of the New World
"The New Heaven and the New Earth"

On October 12, 1992, many celebrations took place around the World acknowledging the 500th anniversary of what was called the "discovery" of the New World by Christopher Columbus. The year 1992 was also the 500th anniversary of the Vision of Our Lady of Guadalupe, and it was the completion of the 500 year cycle of the Mayan and Incan civilizations' calendars. This global focus on the "New World" and "New Beginnings," created an open portal that, for a brief span of time, merged Heaven and Earth. This allowed our Father-Mother God to transfer the Solar Disc of the Twelve-fold Aspect of Deity into the physical axis of Earth. This expanded the Causal Body of Mother Earth from a Seven-fold Planetary Body into a Twelve-fold Solar Body, increasing Her Light a thousand times a thousandfold.

To assist in the transfer of the Solar Disc into physical reality, spiritual groups gathered in Mexico and in South America in the Sacred Foci of the Sun. One group met on the Island of the Sun in Lake Titicaca, Bolivia, the Feminine Polarity of the Sun, and the other spiritual group met at Palenque, Mexico, the Masculine Polarity of the Sun. Throughout that sacred day (October 12, 1992), the two groups invoked the Divine Light of God into the physical plane of Earth. As the Masculine and Feminine Polarity of Solar Light penetrated into the axis of Earth, the Solar Disc was anchored and secured in the ancient focus of the Sun in the District of Heliopolis (the "City of the Sun") in Cairo, Egypt, on the continent of Africa--the dark continent. This caused a slight earthquake in the District of Heliopolis. There had never been an earthquake there before, but the prophecies in Cairo had foretold of a coming earthquake that would one day occur in the "City of the Sun" in Cairo signaling the beginning of the Permanent Golden Age.

After the transfer of the Solar Disc to the physical dimensions of Mother Earth, the next step of Planetary Healing was to raise the frequency and vibration of the dark continent of Africa. With the final two pockets of negativity sealed in Bolivia and South Africa, all was in readiness to draw the Circle of the Sacred Twelve from the anchorage point in the District of the Sun in Heliopolis in Cairo, through all of Africa to the Sacred focus of Table Mountain at the southernmost point of Africa in Cape Town. A spiritual Conference called "Planet in Change" was held in South Africa to build a momentum of Light that would magnetize the Light of the Solar Disc from Cairo through all of Africa to Table Mountain. The entire Elemental Kingdom was prepared to receive the Light, and on October 31, 1992, the Elemental Harvest at Shamballa, the Light of the Solar Disc flashed through Africa returning Her once and for all to a continent of Light.

Now, there is no physical manifestation on Earth that can hold us in darkness other than Humanity's lower human ego which is losing its grip moment by moment.

The Earth has been re-established *permanently* as a Planet of Light, and the New Earth is now being borne. It is our responsibility to become the tangible Light of our Solar Disc and express Limitless Physical Perfection in every aspect of our lives. The effect of this Transfiguration will be exponential, and far sooner than we realize, all Life evolving on Earth will be experiencing the Glories of the "New Heaven and the New Earth." As above, so below.

The following chapters contain specific tools, visualizations, exercises, knowledge and wisdom that, if applied according to the instructions given, will assure your physical transformation.

Again, I want to remind you never to accept anything as Truth just because somebody told you it is so. Read every word carefully and allow it to resonate in your Heart Flame. Ask your Mighty "I AM" Presence to reveal to you if this knowledge is in alignment with your Divine Plan. As long as your Divine Intent is to be the greatest force of good you can possibly be on Earth, with no thought of ego or self-aggrandizement, you will never be led astray. Your God Presence has been anxiously awaiting this Cosmic Moment, when at long last you will reunite with the luminous Presence of your Holy Christ Self and be Transformed into the radiant Being of Light you were originally intended to be.

ALL IS IN READINESS, THE SACRED KNOWL-EDGE IS BEING REVEALED; THE CHOICE IS UP TO YOU!

The cassette tapes to assist you in integrating this chapter into your daily life experience are listed on page 177.

CHAPTER
TWO

TRANSFIGURATION. . .
INTEGRATING OUR HOLY CHRIST SELF
INTO OUR FOUR LOWER BODIES

I want to *strongly emphasize* again the unique opportunity we are being given. In order for this Planet to move into Her rightful spiral of evolution, we must Transmute the miscreation of the human ego and return our physical, etheric, mental and emotional bodies to their rightful owner, our Holy Christ Self. This will result in the Transfiguration of our bodies, which means actually transforming them into *Eternal Youth, Vibrant Health and Radiant Beauty*. Now, because this seems so unbelievable to the masses of Humanity, it is critical that the Lightworkers PROVE this fact by applying the Sacred Knowledge pouring forth from the Realms of Illumined Truth, and rejuvenating and healing our bodies. It is so crucial that there be tangible examples of this process of Transfiguration within Humanity for the masses to witness that there has been a Cosmic Dispensation granted to give super-human assistance to *anyone* who is willing to dedicate their life energies to integrating their Holy Christ Self into their four lower bodies.

This Dispensation means that for every electron of precious life energy we expend in applying the tools of Transfiguration to our daily lives, the entire Company of Heaven will pour forth assistance to amplify our humble efforts the maximum that Cosmic Law will allow. This will *greatly* enhance our effectiveness. Never before have we been given such an incredible opportunity.

The tools of Transfiguration contained within this book have been given to us from the Realms of Illumined Truth. If you will be diligent in the application of these gifts of Sacred Knowledge, you will be amazed at your rapid progress. We have all been truly blessed to receive this information.

As you apply the tools revealed in this book, you will

connect directly with the Divine Mind of God yourself. Then new tools and methods of Transfiguration will be revealed to you directly that will enhance your effectiveness and accelerate your progress.

Remember, this is why we have volunteered to be in embodiment during this Cosmic Moment on Earth. We have been preparing for thousands of years to be able to do this. Every skill, talent, strength and ability we need to succeed in this endeavor is already within us. All we have to do now is apply the tools and DO IT!

Through the miracles of Ascension that have occurred over the past few years, we are connected with our Holy Christ Self at an atomic cellular level, both through our Twelve-fold Solar Spine and our RNA-DNA structures. This means that we are, at long last, capable of drawing directly into our cells and organs the Life Force that will restore our bodies. This Divine Life Force has the ability to create perfect matter and perfect flesh and blood, regardless of the afflictions we might be suffering from. This Transformation and rejuvenation will occur as we effectively integrate our Divine Self into our physical bodies. This will result in the actual restructuring of the atoms and molecules of our cells, thus creating conditions of perfect health, eternal youth and radiant beauty.

I know that the concept of spirit and matter becoming one conflicts with most of our previous understanding, but the Truth is that these two aspects of our Being can and will become one. Our belief in separation, i.e., soul and body, matter and spirit, was a result of the "fall" and it created in us a duality that has prevented our God Self from having full dominion of our four lower bodies. When we again accept that all is Divine and we begin to identify physical substance with God, we will redeem our physical reality and all that is contained within it. We will then experience a tangible fusion of the substance of our Holy Christ Self and our physical bodies.

The exercises contained within this chapter are specifically designed to help us integrate the Divine Light of our Holy Christ Self into the physical substance of our four lower bodies. As we do these exercises daily, according to our inner guidance, we will experience the actual Transfiguration of our physical body.

Transfiguration is a word we've heard used in reference to supernatural, mystical changes in the physical body. Transfiguration is often thought of as an instantaneous influx of Light that transcends the physical body from an Earthly form into a Celestial form. We've sometimes thought of it as a remote possibility for advanced adepts and high initiates, but I don't think we ever really believed it would be a possibility for us. We may have dreamed that in some distant future we would evolve into such advanced souls, but we certainly didn't dare to hope we were ready for Transfiguration right here and right now. The thought seems almost ludicrous in the face of our present Earthly condition. After all, look at our bodies. How many of us are reflecting the perfection of our Holy Christ Self which is actually the Divine Blueprint pulsating at the core of our RNA-DNA patterns. How many of us are emulating Eternal Youth, Vibrant Health, Radiant Beauty, Slim, Firm, Flawless Forms? Not too many, unfortunately. Even those disciplined souls who eat healthy diets, exercise regularly, think positive thoughts and react harmoniously to their daily challenges begin to show signs of aging once they reach their middle years. It appears as though the gradual disintegration of the physical body is a natural process that all of us are subject to if we live in this third dimensional plane. Consequently, when we hear about Transfiguration, which literally means transcending the aging, disease, disintegration and even the death of the physical body, it seems a little far fetched. In actuality, Transfiguration IS available to each and every one of us here and now.

The Earth is in the midst of a unique experiment, and all life abiding upon this Planet is part of the experiment. Regardless of whether or not we fully accept or understand what is happening here, at some level, we have all agreed to participate.

The process that has brought us to this point in Earth's experiment is rather complex, and I have discussed it in detail in my book *Your Time Is At Hand.* For our purposes here, I will briefly explain that our Solar System is in the process of what is known as a Cosmic Inbreath. As the Suns and Planets of a particular Solar System are brought into manifest form, they are breathed out from the Heart of the Universal Source of all Life into the formed primal Light substance of physical reality. As they evolve, they are gradually breathed in, in step-by-step increments, back into the Heart of God. The Divine Fiat has been issued that it is now time for our Solar System to ascend another inbreath closer to the Heart of our Father-Mother God. The Earth and all Her life are being given the opportunity to ascend from the third dimensional frequencies of existence into the Fourth Dimensional frequencies of existence.

This process of creation, the outbreath and the inbreath, has been a natural part of evolution since time began. The thing that makes Earth's part in this natural process a unique experiment is that in order for a Planet to be breathed in to a higher spiral of evolution, it normally must be vibrating at a frequency of Harmony and Balance that is compatible with the new dimensional orbit it is moving into. In the Earth's case, She is not vibrating at the correct frequency.

Never before has a Planet so contaminated with negativity and discord been given the opportunity to move into the next cycle. What normally happens in such a case is that the contaminated planet is left behind during the Divine Inbreath. Then as the Light of its physical Sun is gradually withdrawn, it slowly dies and is eventually dissipated.

The experiment occurring on Earth is an unparalleled act of Mercy and Compassion granted to us by our Father-Mother

God. It is the result of the entire Company of Heaven, literally Galaxies beyond Galaxies and Suns beyond Suns, appealing to our God Parents to invoke Divine Intervention to save this wayward Planet. Whenever there is a display of Divine Love of such tremendous magnitude, Cosmic Law allows dispensations of mercy and forgiveness to be granted that will temporarily set aside the normal rules. In the case of the Earth, a merciful dispensation has been granted. For a brief time, we are being given superhuman assistance to see if we can atone for the misqualification of our precious gift of life and regain our direction. Because of some major vibrational shifts on the Planet and an adjustment of the Spiritual Axis of the Earth, we are now in alignment with the Divine Presence of our Holy Christ Self in a way that we have not been since the "fall of man" aeons ago. Prior to these compassionate influxes of Light, we were evolving on the humanly created wheel of discord and separation. This was a frequency far below what was originally intended for our Earthly experience. On this wheel of discord and separation, often called the wheel of karma, the energies and direction from our Holy Christ Self had to reach us from an oblique angle. Consequently, our communication with our Divine Self was obscure and muted. We actually began to believe that our physical body and our physical environment were all that existed. Once we separated from our Holy Christ Self, our physical bodies began to disintegrate, age and die. This sad scenario became such a prevalent part of our Earthly experience that we came to believe it was natural, and we even believed it was part of the plan. As we acted out of the distorted belief system that aging, disease and death are normal, we effectively perpetuated the problem. Our physical bodies became denser and denser. The Divine Blueprint of perfection that continually pulsates at the core of every electron of our bodies was cloaked in shadow and negativity. The rejuvenating Light of our Holy Christ Selves was blocked, and our cells and organs became gross mutations of what they were originally intended to be.

Now, through the Love and Mercy of God, all of that has changed. We are once again in alignment with our Holy Christ Selves, and it is finally possible to restore our bodies to their original Divine Blueprint, the perfection of our Divine Selves. *This process is Transfiguration.* It will be a little different from what we have come to understand as Transfiguration in the past. It will not, necessarily, be an instantaneous event but rather a gradual restoration and rejuvenation of our bodies. Because the cells of our bodies have been so abused, battered and neglected, they are very weak and vulnerable. If our Holy Christ Self blasted through them with Its full power of Divine Light, our bodies would actually disintegrate.

Our Transfiguration will occur through a merciful, gentle influx of our Holy Christ Self. As we reach up in consciousness and unite with our Holy Christ Self, we tap the Divine Mind of God wherein lies the Illumined Truth that will guide us Lovingly through our process of Transfiguration. The visualizations and exercises revealed in this book have been given to us during this Cosmic Moment as a gift of Love. Blaze them through the Spark of Divinity in your Heart, and if they resonate as Truth for you, use them daily and experience the Joy of your own personal Transfiguration.

The wonderful thing about the Sacred Knowledge flowing to us from the Divine Mind of God is that all we have to do is apply it to our lives and experiment with it, with the Divine Intent of being the most powerful force of good we are capable of being. If our true Heart's desire is to heal ourselves as we Love all life free on this Sweet Earth, our VICTORY is assured!

As we are lifted up, all life is lifted up with us. Our individual Transfiguration will be tangible proof for Humanity that they, too, can ascend out of distorted, pain-wracked bodies into radiant physical bodies of youth and beauty.

I would like to add one cautionary note. This Divine Knowledge has been revealed to us as a Sacred Trust. **For a brief but unknown period of time, we are being given a** window of opportunity to transcend the "fall of Humanity" and all of its miserable ramifications. Let's each listen to the Divine prompting in our Hearts and commit to proving the Law of Transfiguration while still residing on the physical plane of Earth. This will take our continued concentrated efforts, but what a gift it will be, not only to ourselves, but to all life evolving on Earth.

Because of the urgency of the hour, it is imperative that the Lightworkers begin to prove to the masses of Humanity the reality of physical Transformation. As you know, intellectual knowledge is useless if we can't prove it in our physical experience. The only way we ever teach anyone anything is through example, and we are now being asked by our Father-Mother God to accept the greatest (yet most rewarding) challenge we have ever embarked upon. We are being asked to reverse the aging and degeneration process within our physical bodies and return them to the perfection of our Holy Christ Self. We are also being asked to transform our physical lives into the reality of Heaven on Earth.

As mind-boggling as this may seem, what our Father-Mother God is asking of us is the greatest need of the hour on Earth. We have always known that God will not give us more than we have the strength to handle. We may be given a lot of things we would like not to handle, but never more than we can bear. Another aspect of God's compassion is that we are never asked to do anything we are incapable of doing. We have the free will not to do the things we are asked to do, BUT WE

ALWAYS HAVE THE *ABILITY* TO DO THE THINGS WE ARE ASKED TO DO.

Until we actually Ascended through the doorway on January 11, 1992, not even the Company of Heaven knew exactly what the shift in vibration would mean. Everything was contingent on how much purification was accomplished prior to the shift and how far we would move through the "Doorway" during the shift as we began our 20 year spiral into the Fourth Dimension. According to the Realms of Truth, we Ascended beyond even the expectations of Heaven. Now, our next octave of service is being revealed to us.

The veil has been lifted, and if we will each reach up in consciousness, Divine Knowledge will reveal to us just exactly how to utilize the sacred energy now available for physical Transfiguration.

Because this is such a vitally important part of Earth's Ascension, all of Heaven is joining with us in this Holy Endeavor. As we commit our energies to Transforming our physical bodies and our physical realities into God's Perfection, *we will receive the maximum assistance from the Heavenly Realms that Cosmic Law will allow.*

Each of us has been prepared to do this even if we don't consciously remember just yet. We have also volunteered at inner levels to be the examples of the Truth of Transfiguration, or else we wouldn't be receiving this information (in whatever form). Instead of feeling skeptical or overwhelmed, why don't we just begin to Trust? After all, in this endeavor we have everything to gain and nothing to lose.

The way these new Transformational energies are anchored into our lives at this time will set the pattern for the remaining 20 year cycle. Therefore, we are dedicating this Cosmic Moment to anchoring the Light of Limitless Physical Perfection into the everyday lives of Humanity.

Envision that we have been walking the Earth in the limited confines of our caterpillar form. Through the new alignment with our Holy Christ Self, we have entered our cocoon stage. In this stage, in the embrace and safety of our Loving Holy Christ Self, we gradually invoke the Divine Light of God that will allow our physical bodies to integrate with the Divine Blueprint of our Light Bodies, which is recorded in the pre-encoded memory of our RNA-DNA structures. Through this process, we are Transfigured into the Limitless Physical Perfection of our Butterfly form.

MORNING EXERCISES FOR PHYSICAL TRANSFORMATION

STEP ONE

Grounding the Life Force of the Holy Christ Self

The following exercises have been used by adepts in ancient mystery schools for millennia. Their purpose is to enhance our ability to contact our Holy Christ Self and connect with the Divine Mind of God as we ground the Divine energies through our physical body flushing away all frequencies of negativity.

The physical substance of our bodies is now able to hold the voltage of Divine Energy, but we must continually magnetize It into our cells until It is permanently sustained. As we do these exercises, our bodies will be restored to their full capacity for the perfect receptivity and transmission of the *life force* of our Holy Christ Self. As we integrate this Divine Life Force, we will understand, with greater clarity, the difference between what we have erroneously accepted as our limited potential, which terminates in decay and death and our true, unlimited capacity to receive and transmit the Divine Life Force of our

Holy Christ Self. Through this transformed energy state, we will activate the pituitary, pineal, and hypothalamus glands, and our Crown Chakra will awaken according to our individual Divine Plans. This will bring a consciousness of Enlightenment that will eventually transform the Earth and all life abiding upon Her.

To begin this exercise, lie down comfortably on your back with your arms resting gently at your side. It is not important which direction you are actually lying in, but in your mind's eye see your head to the North and your feet to the South.

Breathe deeply for a moment, and feel your body completely relax.

Now, you see the luminous presence of your Holy Christ Self. It is radiantly beautiful and filled with Love. This Divine Presence lies down in the opposite direction at your feet. The soles of your feet are touching the soles of the feet of your Holy Christ Self. Your Holy Christ Self's head is to the South, and Its feet are to the North. As the soles of your feet touch, it enables you to ground the Divine Life Force of Your Holy Christ Self into your physical reality. It allows the Divine Light to spark through your physical body, cutting free all frequencies of negativity.

Now, you see a large Circle of Light being formed around you. It begins at the right of your head and goes clockwise around your body and the body and head of your Holy Christ Self, as It is completed at the right of your head again. This is an invincible "ring pass not of Flame" that prevents anything that is not of the Light from interfering with this Sacred Activity of Light. It is your Solar Disc reverberating with the Twelvefold Causal Body of God, and It is pulsating with the luminous Presence of the Twelve Solar Archangels.

Your vision now ascends upward into a point of infinite Light far above you. You experience this blazing Sun of Light as the Divine Presence and Mind of God.

From this Divine Mind, revelation and inspiration will flash into your daily experience whenever you turn your attention to It. As you focus on this Point of Light high above you, you experience a shaft of Light flashing from the Divine Mind of God into your Third Eye. A second shaft of Light simultaneously flashes into the Third Eye of your Holy Christ Self, thus forming a triangle. This Light penetrates your brain structure, clearing away the shadow of confusion, doubt and fear. It activates your pituitary, pineal and hypothalamus glands and awakens your Crown Chakra of Enlightenment the maximum allowed according to your Divine Plan. The shaft of Light now flashes down through your body and out through your feet. As It does, It sweeps every frequency of negativity, that is in any way, shape or form preventing you from being the Immaculate Concept of your Holy Christ Self, out of your body through your feet. As the negative energy touches the feet of your Holy Christ Self, it is instantly transmuted and returned to the Divine Mind of God for repolarization. (See illustration page 108.)

Now that you have experienced this Sacred Activity of Light, you realize you can invoke It on the Holy Breath, and you repeat the visualization twelve times, drawing one of the Rays of the Twelve-fold Aspect of Deity through you with each breath.

On the *inbreath* a shaft of Light flashes from the Divine Mind of God into your Third Eye and the Third Eye of your Holy Christ Self, forming a triangle. As you continue *breathing in,* this Sacred Light activates the pituitary, pineal and hypothalamus glands, awakens the Crown Chakra and sweeps through your body, cutting free and removing all negativity through your feet, where it is instantly Transmuted as it touches the feet of your Holy Christ Self. As you *exhale,* the energy is returned from the area of your feet straight up into the Divine Mind of God.

This is a sparking activity of Light flashing through you. It is to be done quickly and rhythmically.

Do it first thing in the morning before you get out of bed, and repeat it as often as you like throughout the day. As you go about your day, continue to feel and experience the soles of your feet connecting with the soles of the feet of your Holy Christ Self, Lighting your every step. This Christ connection keeps you open and receptive to the Divine Mind of God, enabling you to receive the Inspiration and Enlightenment that will transform your Life.

Now, repeat the Holy Breath and the visualization twelve times focusing on a different Ray of the Twelve Solar Aspects of Deity with each breath.

Visualization

Breathing in **1st Breath* - The Light from the Divine Mind of God flashes into your Third Eye; It activates the pituitary, pineal and hypothalamus glands and awakens the Crown Chakra. Then, It sweeps through your body and out your feet, removing every trace of negativity. As you exhale, the negativity is instantly transmuted and returned to the Divine Mind of God. *(12 times)*

> * *1st Breath* - Blue Ray of God's Will
> *2nd Breath* - Yellow Ray of Enlightenment
> *3rd Breath* - Pink Ray of Divine Love
> *4th Breath* - White Ray of Purity
> *5th Breath* - Green Ray of Truth
> *6th Breath* - Ruby Ray of Ministering Grace
> *7th Breath* - Violet Ray of Freedom
> *8th Breath* - Aquamarine Ray of Clarity
> *9th Breath* - Magenta Ray of Harmony
> *10th Breath* - Gold Ray of Eternal Peace
> *11th Breath* - Peach Ray of Divine Purpose
> *12th Breath* - Opal Ray of Transformation

After repeating the exercise twelve times, breathe normally. Gently allow this quickening activity of Light to be assimilated into the cells and organs of your body.

STEP TWO

Integrating the Divine Life Force
Into the Physical Body

Now, after the awakening of the Crown Chakra and the purification of our four lower bodies, we are ready to begin the process of integrating our Holy Christ Self into the atomic cellular structure of our physical body.

Remaining in the same position as Step One, we begin to breathe the Divine Life Force of the luminous Presence of our Holy Christ Self in through the soles of our feet; It ascends up through our legs and lower torso into our hands. We activate the Life Force into our hands by affirming "I AM" that "I AM" as we exhale. (See illustration page 109.)

This Breath and visualization are repeated three times.

After securely anchoring the Divine Life Force of our Holy Christ Self into our hands, we then breathe the Divine Light up our arms and middle torso into our Heart. Again, we activate the Life Force into our Heart by affirming **"I AM" that "I AM"** as we exhale.

This breath and visualization are repeated three times.

After securely anchoring the Divine Life Force of our Holy Christ Self into our Heart, we breathe the Divine Light up our upper torso into our throat and head centers. We activate the Life Force simultaneously into our throat center and head centers (the pituitary, pineal and hypothalamus glands) by affirming **"I AM" that "I AM"** as we exhale.

This breath and visualization are also repeated three times.

This activation of the Divine Life Force of our Holy Christ Self into our hands, Heart, throat and head centers will begin to restore to our physical body the power to receive and transmit the eternal life energy which will transform our flesh and blood into living Light. This begins the process of shifting our consciousness so that we will be able to identify physical substance with God.

It is very important that we draw this Divine Life Force into our bodies *every day*. Integration of the Holy Christ Self every morning will enable this Divine Presence to merge with the physical, cellular structures of our cells and organs. This is the eternal food that will allow the Transfiguration of our physical realities. The exercises are each to be done rapidly. Flash each breath into the corresponding part of your body with a sparking, quickening expansion of Light. Realize that the Divine Life Force you are drawing into your cells from your Holy Christ Self is changing the very substance of your body.

STEP THREE

Balancing the Masculine and Feminine Polarities of God in the Physical Body

The Masculine Polarity of God enters our physical body as a shaft of Sapphire Blue Light through the left-brain hemisphere, and it is *physically* transmitted through the electrical meridians into the right side of the body. The Feminine Polarity of God enters our physical body as a shaft of Pink Light through the right-brain hemisphere, and it is *physically* transmitted through the electrical meridians into the left side of the body. As these two polarities of God are blended into perfect balance in our body, they merge into the Violet Transmuting Flame of

Divine Love. This Sacred Fire prepares our flesh and blood to be receptive to increased frequencies of Divine Light, thus accelerating our process of Transfiguration. So, the third step of our Transfiguration exercises involves the amplification of the Masculine and Feminine polarities of God within us.

Remaining in the same position as the previous exercise, we visualize coming down from the infinite point of Light above us, two mighty shafts of Light. One is the Sapphire Blue Light of our Father God, and It enters at an angle through our left-brain hemisphere and passes through the power center of our throat as It blazes into the right side of our body. The second is the Pink Light of our Mother God, and It enters at an angle through our right-brain hemisphere and passes through the power center of our throat as It blazes into the left side of our body. (See illustration page 110.)

Once within the body, these Light Rays blend into the full gathered momentum of the Violet Transmuting Flame. This Divine Light blazes in, through and around every electron of our four lower bodies and prepares every cell and organ to receive more Divine Light with every breath we take.

Again, I want to stress that these exercises of Divine Light are spiritual food for our physical bodies and must be replenished everyday, just as we need to feed our bodies physical nourishment everyday.

STEP FOUR

Preparing the Spine and Brain Centers to Receive More Light

As we move through these exercises, we realize the effect Light and Holy Breath have on the body. This sacred substance not only energizes our blood and changes our mental capacity, but it enables us to commune in a flash with the Divine Mind of our Holy Christ Self as our ability to absorb and transmit

Light increases.

In Step Four, we sit up and cross our legs as we rest our hands gently on our knees with our palms facing upward. We breathe in deeply and visualize a shaft of White Light ascending from the tailbone area at the base of our spine, up our spinal column into the brainstem at the base of our skull. As we exhale, this Light raises the vibratory rate of our spine, and It is absorbed in, through and around our entire spinal column.

On a second breath, we breathe the White Light up into our hypothalamus gland, then into our pituitary gland, then into our pineal gland. As we exhale, the Light raises the vibratory rate of these three glands, and It is absorbed into our three brain centers.

On the third inbreath, the White Light pours out of the third eye between our eyebrows into the palms of our hands. As we exhale, the Light is anchored permanently into our hands, enabling us to bless all the life we touch. (See illustration page 111.)

Step Four is repeated three times.

STEP FIVE

Merging the Cellular Substance of the Physical Body with the Holy Christ Self

In this exercise, we remain sitting with our legs crossed. We place the fingertips of our right and left hands together, and in our mind's eye, we lift our hands into the very Heart of our Father-Mother God. As our hands enter the Heart of God, we breathe in deeply, and we experience a powerful rush of electronic Light flashing into our fingertips and up our arms into our Heart. This Light is vibrating with all of the Twelve Aspects of Deity. It is the blazing, unified forcefield of Light known as the Circle of the Sacred Twelve. As It enters our Heart, It activates our Chakra of Divine Love, then flashes up into our throat center, through our brainstem into the three major glands in our brain (pituitary, pineal and hypothalamus). (See illustration page 112.) Once these three centers are awakened, we exhale and the Light from the Heart of God begins to spin in spiraling circles out from the three brain centers. Through each center, a spiral of twelve blazing circles of Light begins to sweep in a spinning, clockwise motion through our entire brain and head structure. This Divine Light instantly removes the old, obsolete patterns of the lower human ego and replaces them with the Divine Consciousness of our Holy Christ Self. (See illustration page 113)

The physical structures of our head are restored to vibrant health and eternal youth. Our eyesight and hearing are restored to perfection. Our thinking process becomes clear and alert. All traces of aging and disease are transmuted into Light, and we become one with the perfection of our true God Reality.

On the second inbreath, the Circle of the Sacred Twelve flashes down through our spinal column and awakens every electrical meridian in our body. As we exhale, the shaft of Light blazing through our spinal column begins to spin clockwise as It projects out twelve blazing, spiraling circles of Light that sweep through every cell and organ of our physical body, removing every trace of the degeneration of the lower human ego. The frequency of aging, disease or degeneration vibrating in any cell or organ is replaced with the frequency of LIMIT-LESS PHYSICAL PERFECTION of our Holy Christ Self.

As that perfection reverberates into our cellular structures, the spiraling circles of Divine Light continue expanding out into our etheric, mental and emotional bodies. As these vehicles are transformed, the Light expands out further into our environment, transforming our physical realities into Heaven on Earth. (See illustration page 113.)

Step Five is to be done three times in the morning, but it may be repeated as many times as you like throughout the day.

STEP SIX

Activating Our Five Regenerating Elemental Spheres

Step Six is the final exercise in our morning routine for Transfiguration. Now that our vehicles have been cleansed and infused with Light, we need to seal them in the frequency of our Holy Christ Self by activating the five regenerating Elemental Spheres.

In this exercise, we can either physically stand or just visualize ourselves standing.

1. We begin by drawing the unified shaft of Solar Light, known as the Circle of the Sacred Twelve, into the Ether Sphere that pulsates approximately 12 inches above our head.

We breathe the Light into the Spark of Divinity in the center of the Ether Sphere as we affirm:

"I AM" that "I AM".

As we exhale, we experience this Sphere expanding into a radiant Sun. (See illustration page 114.)

The Ether Sphere connects us directly with the Divine Light of our Holy Christ Self.

2. On the second inbreath, we experience a shaft of Light flowing from the Ether Sphere into the Air Sphere pulsating in the area of our throat, and we affirm into the Air Sphere:

"I AM" the breath of Holy Spirit.

As we exhale, we experience the Air Sphere expanding into a radiant Sun.

The Air Sphere seals our **Etheric Body** into the Light Body of our Holy Christ Self.

3. On the third inbreath, we experience a shaft of Light flowing from the Air Sphere into the Fire Sphere pulsating in the area of our mid-chest, and we affirm into the Fire Sphere:

"I AM" the Fire Breath of the Almighty.
As we exhale, we experience the Fire Sphere expanding into a radiant Sun.

The Fire Sphere seals our **Mental Body** into the Light Body of our Holy Christ Self.

4. On the fourth inbreath, we experience a shaft of Light flowing from the Fire Sphere into the Water Sphere pulsating at the base of our spine, and we affirm into the Water Sphere:
"I AM" the Harmony of my true Being.
As we exhale, we experience the Water Sphere expanding into a radiant Sun.

The Water Sphere seals our **Emotional Body** into the Light Body of our Holy Christ Self.

5. On the fifth inbreath, we experience a shaft of Light flowing from the Water Sphere into the Earth Sphere pulsating between our feet, and we affirm into the Earth Sphere:
"I AM" the master of my physical reality.
As we exhale, we experience the Earth Sphere expanding into a radiant Sun.

The Earth Sphere seals our **Physical Body** into the Light Body of our Holy Christ Self.

I know as you read these Six Steps over, it sounds like a lot to do, but remember, we are talking about a fast, quickening of Light sparking through your four lower bodies. In actual time, all Six Steps shouldn't take more than 15 or 20 minutes to complete each morning. That's a pretty short time to spend on LIMITLESS PHYSICAL PERFECTION, isn't it?

After you complete the Sixth Step, gently rise and go about your day, knowing and feeling that you are One with your Holy

Christ Self. Feel that you are totally infused with Divine Solar Life Force and act out of that frequency of perfection with your every thought, word, feeling and action. You will be amazed at how much easier your life flows.

Remember, this is going to be a gradual process, and your *daily* exercises and the *continual* focusing of your attention on your Holy Christ Self are *imperative* to your success.

The price of Freedom is Eternal Vigilance. I promise you there will be nothing you can do that will be more worth your while than becoming One with your Holy Christ Self.

As we open to the Divine Mind of God, we begin to see clearly how very simple Transfiguration really is. It is actually just a slight adjustment in our awareness. Now that we are grounded with our Holy Christ Self and open to the Divine Mind of God, we can, with every breath we take, be a powerful force of Light on this Sweet Earth. All we have to do is be cognizant of the opportunities being presented to us. Often people feel that they have to be doing something "spiritual" in order to add to the Light of the world, but with a slight adjustment in perception, they will realize everything they do can be spiritual.

It is up to us to magnetize the Divine Life Force into the everyday lives of Humanity that will result in not only our own Transfiguration, but the Transfiguration of all life evolving on Earth as well.

Through the power of our thoughts, words, feelings and actions, we are, with every breath we take, either adding to the Light of the world or the shadow. If we will continually hold in our minds and energize with our feelings, the glorious vision of the Earth transformed, we will help greatly in bringing about Her Transfiguration. For example...

1. *As you walk through the grocery store, invoke a Ray of Healing Light into every morsel of food. Ask that the Healing Light expand through every bite of food that is consumed on the entire planet that day.*
2. *Every time you take a drink of water, consecrate every drop of water on Earth with the Violet Light of Transmutation.*
3. *As you clean your home, invoke a Ray of Comfort and Divine Love into every home on Earth.*
4. *When you drive your car, envision a forcefield of Protection around your car and every car.*
5. *As you fill your car with gas, transmute the pollution it will release, as well as all pollution on Earth, by invoking the Violet Fire into it.*
6. *When you interact with your family, invoke the Harmony of Divine Family Life through all families.*
7. *When you visit a hospital, magnetize Healing into the physical bodies of all the infirmed.*
8. *When you take a breath, bless the air.*
9. *When you pick a flower, bless all of nature.*
10. *When you see the Sun, bless God.*

Be creative. These are just a very few suggestions to give you an idea how your everyday activities can be expanded through your Christ Presence into a global service. Each morning ask yourself **"How today can I expand the Light of God on Earth?"** You will be amazed at how many opportunities begin to pop into your head, opportunities that have always been there, that you just didn't recognize because of being so immersed in the negativity of the "old earth" instead of having the focus of your attention on the LIMITLESS PHYSICAL PERFECTION of the **New Earth!**

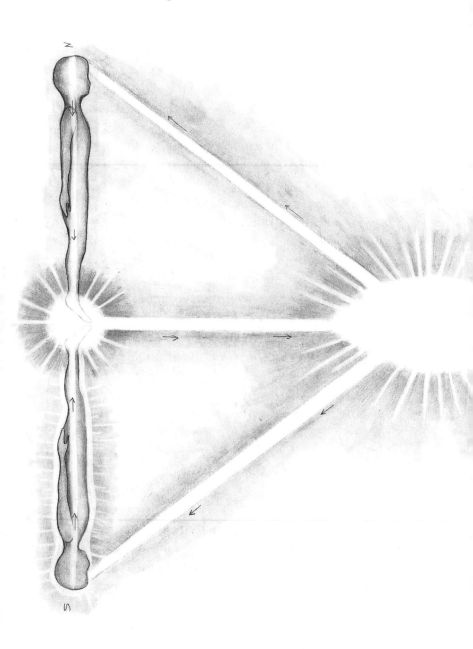

**MORNING EXERCISE
STEP ONE**

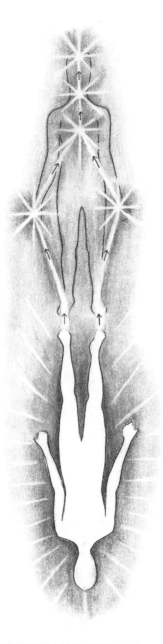

**MORNING EXERCISE
STEP TWO**

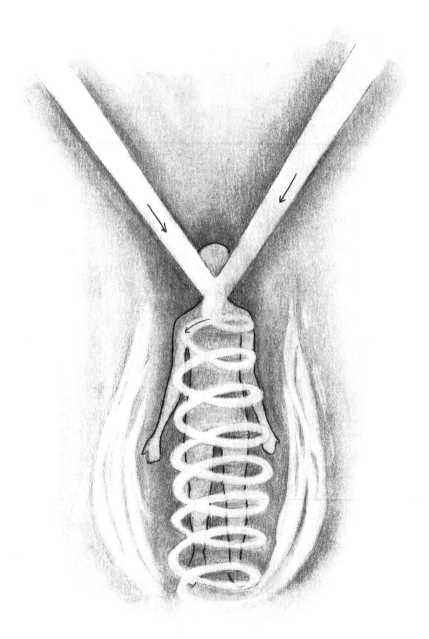

**MORNING EXERCISE
STEP THREE**

**MORNING EXERCISE
STEP FOUR**

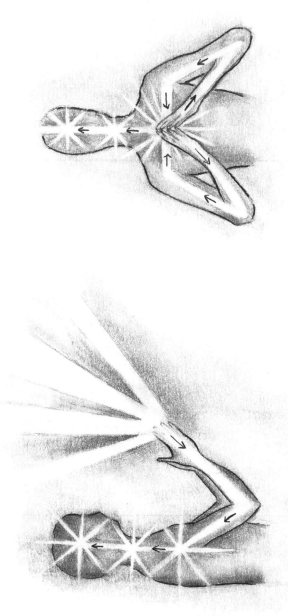

MORNING EXERCISE
STEP FIVE

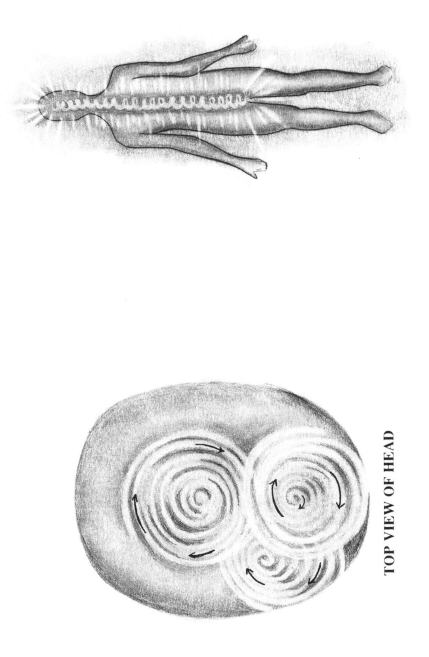

TOP VIEW OF HEAD

**MORNING EXERCISE
STEP FIVE**

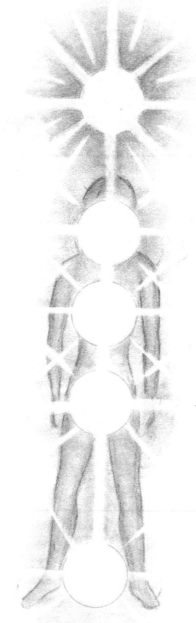

ETHER SPHERE

AIR SPHERE

FIRE SPHERE

WATER SPHERE

EARTH SPHERE

**MORNING EXERCISE
STEP SIX**

EVENING EXERCISES FOR
PHYSICAL TRANSFORMATION

The evening exercises should be done just before retiring. Whatever we focus on before going to sleep, we take into our subconscious. These exercises are designed to give the intelligence of our body food to work with during the night so that our Transfiguration process is an ongoing 24 hour activity of Light. Follow the sequence given here, and then allow yourself to fall into a beautifully peaceful sleep.

STEP ONE

Cleansing Exercise

Stand in your room and call the Violet Transmuting Flame into action in, through and around you for at least nine feet in every direction. Raise your hands, and ask your Higher Self, your God Presence, to qualify your hands with the Purifying Power of the Violet Transmuting Flame. Visualize your hands blazing with Violet Light--pulsating as Amethyst Suns.

Then, starting at your head, pass your hands down over your body to the feet, taking in as much of the body surface as you can reach with your hands. Envision that your hands are mighty magnets, pulling every electron of negativity out of your body.

Now, with the left hand, sweep down over the right shoulder, arm and hand, and with the right hand, give the left shoulder, arm and hand the same treatment.

Repeat this activity in its entirety four times, once for each of the four lower vehicles (physical, etheric, mental and emotional). Periodically shake your hands from the wrist to cast off the heavy, discordant energy that is being removed from your bodies, and visualize the negative energy being Transmuted in the surrounding Violet Fire.

If not just yet, eventually you will be able to see with the inner sight what takes place during this exercise. In the first part of the exercise, it is as though a close fitting garment of dark substance is being removed from the body with the hands. This is real substance--with actual color, vibration and feeling, created through the misuse of energy throughout our Earthly sojourn. The second time you go over the body, the "garment" removed is of a gray substance. The third time, even lighter. The fourth time, even lighter. Day after day, as you proceed with the exercise, this astral substance becomes lighter and lighter in color and texture until it is entirely removed from the body.

On completion of the exercise, visualize the Violet Transmuting Flame expanding through your Heart Flame, flooding the entire Planet and affirm with deep feeling...

Beloved Presence of God in me...EXPAND! EXPAND! AND INTENSIFY DAILY THE MIGHTIEST ACTION OF VIOLET FIRE in, through and around every electron that makes up the atoms of my emotional, mental, etheric and physical vehicles until they outpicture the God Perfection which Thou art!
(Repeat three times)

In the Name of the Almighty Presence of God "I AM" and the Creative Fire pulsating in every human Heart...Beloved Presence of God "I AM" in me and that of all Humanity...

SATURATE MY FEELING WORLD WITH THE VIOLET TRANSMUTING FLAME (three times)

SATURATE MY MENTAL WORLD WITH THE VIOLET TRANSMUTING FLAME (three times)

SATURATE MY ETHERIC WORLD WITH THE VIOLET TRANSMUTING FLAME (three times)

SATURATE MY PHYSICAL WORLD WITH THE VIOLET TRANSMUTING FLAME (three times)

In God's Most Holy Name "I AM".

STEP TWO

Youthing Violet Fire

After the cleansing exercise, lie down and allow your body to completely relax.

One of the most powerful forces of aging is gravity. This constant downward pull toward the center of the Earth causes all of the cells and organs of our physical body to begin to droop and eventually sag. This Youthing Violet Fire exercise is specifically designed to reverse the forces of gravity on the body and give the cells and organs of our body an opportunity to return to their normal youthful state. It is a very simple, but very effective exercise.

Once the cells of our body have been cleansed of all of the day's effluvia by the application of the Cleansing Exercise, we lie down and invoke, through the Presence of God "I AM", the most powerful force of the Violet Transmuting Flame we can withstand.

We visualize this magnificent Amethyst Flame spiraling up from the center of the Earth into the bottom of our feet. It spins in a clockwise motion with a powerful whirling force. As It begins to ascend up through our feet and ankles, we experience this Sacred Violet Fire actually reversing the effect of gravity on our body. As It spins in, through and around the electrons in our feet and ankles, they are uplifted and strengthened.

This spinning whirlwind of Violet Fire continues to ascend up our body. It blazes into our calves, knees, thighs, hips, abdomen, upper torso, chest and shoulders. It expands into our arms and hands, then ascends into our neck and fills our entire head structure. (See illustration page 134.)

All of our bodily functions that promote Eternal Youth, Radiant Beauty and Vibrant Health are activated and restored to perfection. The flexibility, elasticity and moisture of Eternal Youth are restored to each cell.

By the time the Violet Flame reaches the top of our head, every single cell and organ of our body is pulsating with the youthing effects of this Sacred Fire. Every cell is uplifted and purified.

Our Holy Christ Self now projects the Divine Blueprint of Eternal Youth, Vibrant Health, Radiant Beauty, Slim, Firm, Flawless Form clearly onto the RNA-DNA patterns of every cell. We feel the buoyancy of our physical body vibrantly alive and rejoicing in the radiance of new found youth, and we affirm with deep feeling...

In the full power of the Presence of God anchored in my Heart, I ask that this Youthing Violet Fire continue to blaze up through my four lower vehicles throughout the entire night, increasing Its rejuvenating, youthing power moment to moment with every breath I take.

STEP THREE

Restoring Vibrant Health and Eternal Youth to the Systems and Organs of the Body

Now that the pressure of gravity and aging has been lifted from the cells and organs of our body, we can more easily accelerate the vibratory rate of each system to its perfect function.

In this exercise, we again visualize the Violet Transmuting Flame flowing into our hands until they become blazing Amethyst Suns.

The left hand is raised up into the Heart of God, palm up, receiving the full power of Transfiguration. The right hand is used as a powerful transmitter, projecting the Divine Light of Transfiguration into the atoms and molecules of our physical body.

We begin by placing our right hand on our navel, palm

down. Then, we slowly move our right hand in clockwise circles that gradually become larger and larger until the final circle is drawn from the very top of our torso at our neck, to the bottom of our torso at our pubic bone. Once the largest circle is drawn, we return our right hand to our navel and begin drawing the circles again. (See illustration page 135.)

This entire process is repeated *nine times*.

As our right hand is slowly passing in circles over our body, we visualize a tremendous shaft of Light blazing through the palm of our hand into our body. This shaft of Transfiguring Light, which is comprised of all Twelve Solar Rays of Deity, passes completely through our body. As It penetrates into every cell, gland, organ, system and function of our body, It instantly cuts free and removes every trace of aging, disease, deterioration, malfunction, decay or deformity of any kind.

Every system of our body is rejuvenated. The Divine Light blazes through the:

> Chakra System
> Respiratory System
> Circulatory System
> Digestive System
> Elimination System
> Reproductive System
> Glandular System
> Skeletal System
> Nervous System
> Lymphatic System
> Muscular System
> Fat System
> Skin, Hair and Nails
> Eyes, Ears, Nose and Mouth

Each system is rejuvenated, purified and restored to vibrant health and eternal youth through this exercise of Divine Light.

Continue doing the exercise now until you have completed

the series of circles nine times, then progress to the next exercise.

STEP FOUR

Hosanna Christ Consciousness Prayer

Now that we have purified the cells and organs of our body and filled them with the youthing Divine Blueprint of our Holy Christ Self, we need to permanently clear the cause and core of aging and disease. The following symbol and affirmation were given to the Lightworkers to help us cut ourselves free from lines of force that are keeping us bound to the distortion of the past. This is accomplished by using the power of Sacred Geometry and the power of the spoken word.

Hosannna Christ Consciousness Symbol

In your mind's eye, draw this sacred symbol over your body and then affirm the following decree with deep feeling...

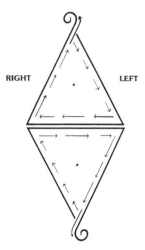

Hosanna Healing Prayer

As the Name, Power and Authority of the Beloved Presence of God "I AM"...I call to to you now, Beloved Archangel Michael and the Angels of Power, place 999 billion 3 multiplex of the Hosanna Christ Consciousness Symbol in, through and around the forcefield of my being and Lovingly cut free all cords, ties, hooks and attachments that bind me in any way, shape or form to the aging, disease, degeneration and death of my physical body. Cut free every frequency of vibration that is less than Limitless Physical Perfection in my four lower bodies and my physical reality.

Intensify this Sacred Symbol to the 999th Power, and expand this activity of Freeing Light through ALL planes and ALL dimensions, on ALL levels from ALL lifetimes multidimensionally. Release me NOW and forever from the cause, core, effect, record, memory and momentum of aging, disease, degeneration and death.

ANGELS OF THE VIOLET FIRE, come forth now, and Transmute instantly, through the power of the Violet Transmuting Flame, all the negative energy being cut free by Archangel Michael and the Angels of Power.

Blaze, Blaze, Blaze the Violet Flame through all beliefs, attitudes, concepts and acceptance of the illusion of aging, disease, degeneration and death. Replace these distorted thoughtforms of the lower human ego with the Illumined Truth of Limitless Physical Perfection...Eternal Youth, Vibrant Health and Radiant Beauty.

ANGELS OF UNCONDITIONAL LOVE, TRUTH, TRANSFIGURATION, TRANSFORMATION, HEALING,

*FORGIVENESS, HOPE, TRUST, PROSPERITY, ABUN-
DANCE, HARMONY, BALANCE, FAITH, UNDERSTAND-
ING, PEACE, JOY, HAPPINESS AND VICTORY come forth
now, and fill every electron of my four lower bodies with your
resplendent Divine Qualities.*

*Beloved Legions of Light, I thank you, and I accept that
this activity of Light has been permanently established with
full power, to be eternally self-sustained, increasing daily and
hourly, moment to moment, with every breath I take, the
maximum that Cosmic Law will allow.*

*I accept this call fulfilled through the Presence of God "I
AM"!!!*

So Be It!

Note: This decree can be modified to address any challenge
you are going through; just insert what you would like to be
cut free from in the appropriate place.

STEP FIVE

Opening the Physical Vehicles to the Twelve-Fold Aspect of Deity

Our evening purification is now complete, and we are ready to receive the greatest influx of Divine Light our God Presence will allow.

This exercise actually creates a pathway of Light that passes from Divine Realms of Perfection through our Solar Chakra System into our four lower bodies. The Chakras are the only system that interpenetrates all four of the lower bodies, and this exercise powerfully infuses the Twelve-fold Aspect of Deity into our bodies at an atomic cellular level, greatly increasing our capacity to absorb Light. This exercise involves a series of spirals. The spirals begin at the nape of the neck and are drawn over the head from back to front, piercing into each of the Twelve Solar Chakras, beginning with the Crown Chakra and ending with the Root Chakra. Each spiral is completed on an inbreath, then we exhale quickly before beginning the next spiral. (See illustration page 136.)

We first visualize a mighty shaft of the unified forcefield of the Twelve-fold Aspect of Deity pouring forth from the Heart of God into our Crown Chakra.

This Divine Light passes into the Master Head Center, which is our hypothalamus gland at the base of our skull. It then passes out the nape of our neck at the back of our head and begins a series of 12 spirals through our body. First the shaft of Light passes over the head into the Crown Chakra of Enlightenment creating the first spiral circle. It then passes out the back of the head and circles back over the head, entering the Third Eye Chakra of Truth. This creates the second spiral. The shaft of Light again passes out the back of the head and re-enters the body at the point of the Clarity Chakra in the area of our nose. This is the third spiral. Next, the Light passes out the back of the head and passes over the head as It enters the Throat Chakra of Divine Will. This is the fourth spiral. The fifth spiral passes over the head and enters at the midpoint between the Throat and Heart Chakras; this is the Chakra of Harmony. The sixth spiral passes out the back over the head and enters the Heart Chakra of Divine Love from the front. The seventh spiral passes out of the back and over the head as it enters the Chakra of Eternal Peace just below the Heart. The eighth spiral enters the Chakra of Divine Purpose located just above the solar plexus. The ninth spiral enters the Solar Plexus Chakra of Ministering Grace. The tenth spiral enters the Central Chakra of Freedom located in the mid-abdomen. The eleventh spiral enters the Chakra of Transformation located below the mid-abdomen and the twelfth and final spiral enters the Root Chakra of Purity at the base of the spine.

This activity of cutting a spiraling pathway of Solar Light through our four lower bodies, creates open portals that allow the Divine Light of God to easily flow through our Solar Spine into our four lower bodies and subsequently, into our environment and world. Light has always passed through our bodies into the world, but it has been contaminated and blocked by the denseness of our bodies. Now, our bodies are becoming rarified and purified. Consequently, these tools of Transfiguration that enable us to greatly expand the Light passing through us can now be revealed to us.

STEP SIX

Transforming the Four Lower Bodies into the Immaculate Concept of the Holy Christ Self

This activity is dedicated to re-establishing the Divine Blueprint...the Immaculate Concept...within your physical, etheric, mental and emotional vehicles.

Through this exercise, you will energize each vehicle until the pulsating force of the Holy Christ Self is within that vehicle, thus regenerating health, beauty, eternal youth and order physically, etherically, mentally and emotionally.

To begin...lie down comfortably with your arms and legs uncrossed and your spine as straight as possible. Breathe in deeply, and as you exhale, completely relax and gently close your eyes. Feel yourself enveloped in an invincible Forcefield of Protection which prevents anything not of the Light from interfering with this sacred activity. This is a journey in consciousness that will physically manifest through the power of your true God Reality "I AM".

In projected consciousness, visualize yourself standing before a magnificent Crystalline Temple of Healing in the Realms of Illumined Truth. You ascend the steps and pass through the massive doors. You pass through the alabaster hallway and enter the sacred, central chamber. As you stand within the central chamber, you notice that there are four surrounding chambers at the cardinal points. Pulsating in the center of the central chamber is a radiant crystal Lotus Blossom, and blazing within the center of the Lotus Blossom is a crystalline Madonna Blue Flame with a White aura. It is the Flame of the Immaculate Concept.

An Angelic Being beckons you, and you enter the crystalline Lotus Blossom and stand within the scintillating essence of the Flame of the Immaculate Concept. You begin to experience the vibratory rate of your four lower bodies being accelerated. Your consciousness is rising, and you perceive, more clearly than ever before, the Divine Blueprint for each of your vehicles.

Pouring forth now from the very Heart of God is a tremendous Ray of Light that is pulsating with the God Qualities of Restoration, Transformation, Healing, Eternal Youth and Radiant Beauty. This shaft of Light enters the Flame of the Immaculate Concept, and then expands out to each of the outer chambers at the cardinal points which are dedicated specifically to one of the four lower vehicles of your life's expression.

You now consciously project your emotional body and all of your feelings into the chamber at the cardinal point to the East. God's Holy Light begins blazing in, through and around this vehicle, transmuting every trace of imbalance. Your God Presence now projects the Divine Blueprint for your etheric body through this vehicle, and it begins pulsating as a Light Pattern, transforming this vehicle instantly into the Immaculate Concept of your Holy Christ Self.

You now consciously project your mental body and all of your thoughts into the chamber at the cardinal point to the West. God's Holy Light begins blazing in, through and around this vehicle, transmuting every trace of imbalance. Your God Presence now projects the Divine Blueprint for your mental body through this vehicle, and it begins pulsating as a Light Pattern, transforming this vehicle instantly into the Immaculate Concept of your Holy Christ Self.

You now consciously project your etheric body and all of your memories and records of the past into the chamber at the cardinal point to the North. God's Holy Light begins blazing in, through and around this vehicle, transmuting every trace of imbalance. Your God Presence now projects the Divine Blueprint for your etheric body through this vehicle, and it begins pulsating as a Light Pattern, transforming this vehicle instantly into the Immaculate Concept of your Holy Christ Self.

You now consciously project your physical body, every cell, atom, gland, muscle, organ and function, into the chamber at the cardinal point to the South. God's Holy Light begins blazing in, through and around this vehicle, transmuting every trace of imbalance. Your God Presence now projects the Divine Blueprint for your physical body through this vehicle, and it begins pulsating as a Light Pattern, transforming this vehicle instantly into the Immaculate Concept of your Holy Christ Self.

Now, one by one, you magnetize these purified, balanced vehicles back into the Flame of the Immaculate Concept where they are brought into perfect alignment: first the physical, then the etheric, then the mental, then the emotional. Your vehicles are now balanced, and once again returned to the service of your God Presence "I AM" and your Holy Christ Self.

Sealing Affirmation

"I AM" the Immaculate Concept (the Divine Blueprint) of my true God Reality.

"I AM" a radiant Being of Light.

"I AM" Eternally Youthful, Vibrantly Healthy, Radiantly Beautiful--Slim, Firm, Flawless form. I love my body and nourish it with perfect eating and drinking habits, deep breathing, fresh air, sunshine and exercise.

"I AM" God In Action on Earth, and with every breath I take "I AM" expanding the Light of the World.

"I AM" consciously aware of my Divine Plan, and "I AM" fulfilling every aspect of it Perfectly.

"I AM" daily and hourly open and receptive to the flow of God's Abundance. "I AM" Eternally Financially Free.

All of my relationships pulsate with the essence of Divine Love and Reverence for all Life. They are rewarding, inspiring, fulfilling, wonderful and glorious.

My work fills my Life with a sense of Joy and Accomplishment. Everyday "I AM" richly rewarded creatively and financially.

Each day I commune with the Angels and the Elementals; we walk hand-in-hand in Unity as we transform this Sweet Earth into Freedom's Holy Star--Heaven on Earth.

Every man, woman and child on Earth is one with their true God Reality. Each one expresses only Reverence for all Life.

Divine Government Rules every nation. Divine Love, Eternal Peace, Abounding Joy and Happiness, Prosperity, Victorious Accomplishment and God's Will are the order of the New Day on Earth!

Through the Flaming Presence of God anchored in my Heart,
I ask that this transforming activity of Light be maintained,
eternally self-sustained, daily and hourly increased moment
by moment until each of my four lower vehicles is outpicturing
the perfection ordained for me, and "I AM" wholly Ascended
and Free.

It is Done!
So Be It! "I AM"
BE STILL AND KNOW THAT "I AM" GOD

STEP SEVEN

The Rosary of the New Age of Spiritual Freedom

Our four lower bodies and our spinal column are now
aligned, purified and receptive for our final evening exercise.

This exercise is a Divine Gift that is designed to not only
greatly expand the Light of the world, but to seal our bodies
permanently in the Divine Blueprint of Eternal Youth, Vibrant
Health and Radiant Beauty. A special gift has been given to us
to help us integrate the Sacred Fire of Creation now pouring
through our four lower bodies from the Twelve-fold Solar
Spine of our God Presence "I AM". How well we integrate this
Light will set the tone for our passage into the Octaves of
Limitless Physical Perfection we have now embarked upon.

Beloved Mother Mary, who represents the Divine Mother
Principle on Earth, has given us a sacred gift to enhance our
ability to Ascend into the Realm of Limitless Physical Perfection.

At the inception of the last Age, the Christian Dispensation,
Beloved Mother Mary volunteered to come to Earth in a
physical body to offer Her vehicle as the open door through

which the Avatar of that Age, Beloved Jesus, would embody in human form.

She had been trained at inner levels for centures of time on the principles of holding the Immaculate Concept, which is the Divine Blueprint for all manifest form. As She entered the physical plane, She was entrusted with the Immaculate Concept of the Divine Plan for Beloved Jesus. Every detail of His sacred mission on Earth was recorded in Mother Mary's Heart Flame, and with every breath She took during Her Earthly sojourn, She nourished and protected that plan. With the clear vision of His Divine Plan held before Him through the concentrated efforts of Mother Mary, Jesus' mission was brought to fruition with Victorious Accomplishment. Even in the face of the most terrifying adversity, Jesus passed through His Earthly initiations into Christhood Victoriously.

As Mother Mary walked down from the hill at Golgotha after the crucifixion of Her Beloved Son, She said, "What I have done for you, my Son, I now do for all mankind." At that moment, Mother Mary's Divine service expanded from holding the Immaculate Concept for one Avatar-Christed Being to holding the Immaculate Concept for every man, woman and child evolving on Earth until each one likewise attains the Christed state of Being and again reclaims his/her natural birthright as a Son or Daughter of God, thus Healing, once and for all, our self-inflicted separation from God.

At the inception of this New Age, the Permanent Golden Age of Spiritual Freedom, Beloved Mother Mary is again making Her presence known. She is cradling this Sweet Earth in Her Heart Flame and has asked that each of us enhance Her ability to assist the Earth and all life evolving here by balancing Her efforts. Cosmic Law states that the call for assistance must come from the realm where the assistance is needed and that the energy pouring forth from the Heavenly Realms must be balanced by Humanity's energy.

Mother Mary's symbol has always been a white rose of purity. In the past Age, She revealed to the consciousness of Humanity a prayer that would assist in balancing Her efforts to help the evolutions of Earth. This prayer was called "The Rosary."

Now, during this Cosmic Moment of planetary transformation when Mother Mary's service to Earth has been expanded to holding the Immaculate Concept for every particle of life, She again reveals to us a prayer that will increase in power a thousand times a thousandfold each time it is recited. This invocation of unprecedented power will allow the Immaculate Concept for Planet Earth, the Divine Blueprint being held within the Mind of God, to quickly manifest. She has assured us that, as we recite this sacred prayer, our individual lives will begin to reflect clearly our Divine Purpose and reason for being. The illusion of the third dimensional plane that has trapped us in lack and limitation will be dissipated, and the reality of our Divine Heritage--Heaven on Earth--will be revealed.

Each of us must go within to the Presence of God pulsating in our Hearts and evaluate, according to our wisdom and our understanding, the opportunity at hand. Then, in deep humility and gratitude, we shall recite this sacred prayer according to our inner direction.

The Rosary of the New Age
*Hail Mother, full of Grace, the Lord is with Thee.
Blessed art Thou amongst women, and Blessed is the
fruit of Thy womb "I AM".
Hold for us NOW the immaculate Concept of our
true God Reality from this moment unto our Eternal
Ascension in the Light.
"I AM" that "I AM".

The preceding prayer is repeated 12 times, once for each of the Rays of the Twelve Solar Aspects of Deity. As each "Hail Mother..." is stated, visualize the color and qualities of the corresponding Ray entering your Heart and flooding through you to bathe the Planet (see chart page 133).

After reciting the "Hail Mother..." 12 times, focusing on a different Solar Aspect each time, repeat the following affirmation three times:

"I AM" the Immaculate Concept of my true God Reality, NOW made manifest and sustained by Grace.

At the conclusion of the entire series, the energy is sealed and permanently sustained by decreeing:

It is done! So be it! "I AM"!

THE ROSARY OF THE NEW AGE

Recite "Hail Mother"	Solar Aspect	Solar Archangels	Solar Archaii	Color	Qualities
1st Time	1st Ray	Michael	Faith	Blue	God's Will
2nd Time	2nd Ray	Jophiel	Constance	Yellow	Enlightenment
3rd Time	3rd Ray	Chamuel	Charity	Pink	Divine Love
4th Time	4th Ray	Gabriel	Hope	White	Purity
5th Time	5th Ray	Raphael	Mother Mary	Green	Truth
6th Time	6th Ray	Uriel	Donna Grace	Ruby	Ministering Grace
7th Time	7th Ray	Zadkiel	Holy Amethyst	Violet	Freedom
8th Time	8th Ray	Aquariel	Clarity	Aquamarine	Clarity
9th Time	9th Ray	Anthriel	Harmony	Magenta	Harmony
10th Time	10th Ray	Valeoel	Peace	Gold	Eternal Peace
11th Time	11th Ray	Perpetiel	Joy	Peach	Divine Purpose
12th Time	12th Ray	Omniel	Opalessence	Opal	Transformation

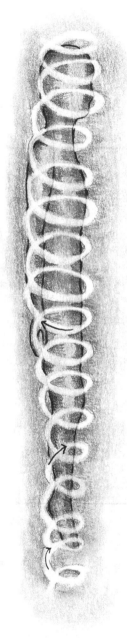

**EVENING EXERCISE
STEP TWO**

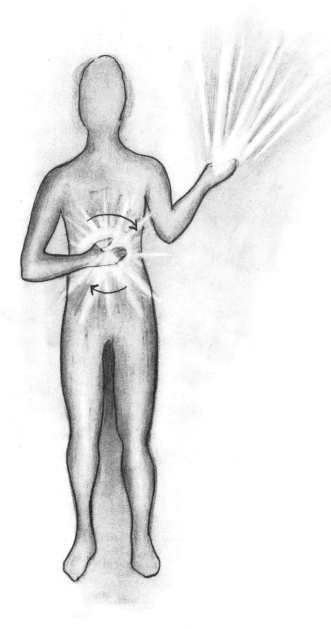

**EVENING EXERCISE
STEP THREE**

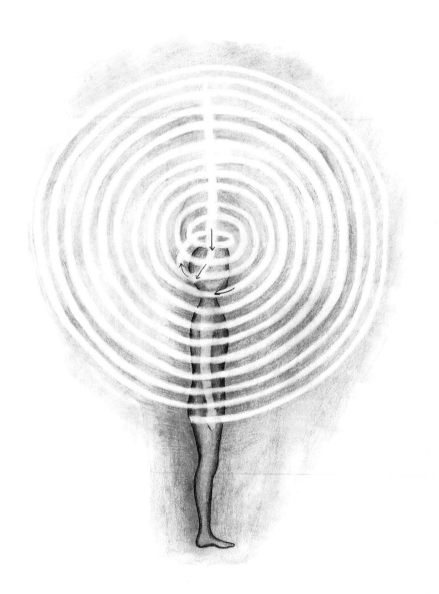

EVENING EXERCISE
STEP FIVE

DIVINE MOTHER

As the blessed energies of our Father/Mother God are being balanced on Earth, we are beginning to feel, from the depths of our being the nurturing Mother's Love that is flowing through our Hearts. As this occurs, we are unified with the exquisite energy of our Earthly Mothers. The following poem is a beautiful expression of that Motherly Love as it echos through time. It was written by my beloved friend, Mary Engel.

To My Youngest Child Marigrace Sophia:

I am an arc in time.

Ancient mothers fill the baskets that I hold, and swing
across a firmament of unmarked skies to the farthest
reaches of my Earth time
where you stand
and thrust the basket into your reluctant arms.

I see your eyes upon the distant mountain
Vistas of your path illumined by Aquarian Moon,
the path where first I set your baby feet and whispered
through your starry dreams of New Worlds I know, but
may not find.

You are the future as once was I
And so were those who went before me too
Who filled their little scan
with women's hopes, with scars of many knowings.
They pass along their treasured dishes, crystal vases,
bowls,
triumphant gifts to mark their celebrations
to set enthroned on ecru lace
in polished wood and beveled glass.

LISTEN!
Trays of gold rimmed glasses--beer and ginger ale and
welcome ices
tinkle mid the cricket sounds
and white rose fragrances of a summer night.
Soft exclaiming voices blend with
creaking porch swings
behind the hallmark of Wisteria
half lit by lamp and half by moon.

Ladies, ladies sitting, hoping, waiting and remembering,
holding essence in themselves
watching gates along the way and cousins
entering
and porch lights flickering among the leaves.
horses and carriages along the cobble stones bring
papas home and doctors, priests, and morning milk and
other things.

They drift back into flags and wars and sigh for
stalwarts who marched away to righteous drumbeats
to fight the last war ever--
Again, and then again, and yet again.
They still half listen for their returning steps.

Ladies mark their calendars...confessions, ice man
comes, coal delivered, pump goes dry, gas lights
changed, telephones installed, births and passings.

Memories fade, they peer back into faces neatly set in
musty covered books
Ah yes, they are here, the many mothers. Whose eyes
are these? Whose Brow? Whose stance does manifest
the secret genes we carry filed within our mortal frames?

Look at those hands, trained to ephemeral pleasures of
piano, and of violin, but too, the fashioning of towels
and quilts and lacy forms, enduring stuff that ladies keep
about that speaks their love, their care. Into all the
movements of the aging wrists they weave the colors
and the codings of their days. Baby fingers making
horserein on their tiny spools cross stitch into the
intricacies they now weave into their enduring works,
wisdom of continuity and knowing and remembrance
of wickered gardens, green awninged summer days
of flowered tea parties and expectant hush and awe of
baby showers, of grandiose home weddings and of
rainy afternoons with giggling schoolgirls pouring
lemonade and making fudge--of taffy pulls--
Of Christmas lists and wraps and glitter, of joyous bright
decked pine and holly wreaths or solemn white and
violet crepes upon the carved oak front hall doors,
of clotheslines strung with proud embroidered cotton,
of gleaming silver on lacy mats on aristocratic damask.

Pride and passion in days that were a prelude and finale
set in one.

Woolen socks from tiny snow-cold feet, their darned
patches little lumps of ice
thawing into blanketed cushions stuffed into wide oven
door, small fingers clasping steamy cups of broth, snow-
babies swaddled in patchwork cocoons, drift off to naps
and icicles and Jack Frost dreams.

They grew before these mirrors and set their treasured
rings and pins in ribboned boxes in drawers of polished
wood that Papa made, colognes and calling cards and
bordered notes upon the marbled surfaces. Hatpins,

hairpins waiting in their porcelain dishes. Morning sunlight through white organdy, church bells and fresh
flowers sent by swains and gracefully placed before Our
Lady as with all of life.

Crystal rosaries and sweet bisque angel faces. Prayer
books aburst with holy cards to witness morn and
evening prayers. Feather beds and feathering quilts and
pillows long and soft. Kitchen smell of coffee and of
kuchen. Alsatian onions and potatoes and hearty soups
and Sunday lamb and Christmas chicken. Bread
toasted on coal stoves and apple dumplings. Garden
mint and nameless wondrous herbs that comforted
and healed.

Through it all, the breeze that spoke of home beyond,
that fondled lace in the bay windows and carried lily
of the valley angel whispers through the rooms, the
breeze that came as household devas traced the
family nest.

Ancient mothers, somehow virgins all, those who
birthed and those who held the threads of timeless love
and sought their places and nurtured all.
What matters who brought forth the child? It is our line
and all we carried on, we pass. We give our names, our
blessings, our woven ties. Through us you know of
daily strengths, of gracious ways. We are your island,
your Avalon in the turbulence of now.

And so their baskets fill with things
Women, ancient mothers speak through things--their
touch, their understanding fortitude locked in
substance. So when the earthly form has faded and the

face within the frame wakes no sighs of recognition--
their artistry created still endures--locked in every stitch
and loop their love they pass to you.
So I bring this basket now from far beyond
from all those fading faces that you never knew
One day I shall be one of them.
No matter that,
I know of finer fields to sow, my weavings of the mind
and heart,
A mission ends to pass along the roots, and so I do,
What shall be now I leave to you.

DIVINE LOVE

The purpose of our Lives is to Glorify the flesh and Glorify the Earth, raising the vibrations of physical matter until the entire Planet becomes TRANSFIGURED into Fourth Dimensional frequencies, thus Ascending Spiritually on Its return journey to the Father-Mother God.

Through Divine Love and Wisdom and through service to our fellow human beings, our bodies become Purified--literally refined and rarefied.

Transfiguration occurs when the God Self, pulsating in our Hearts, becomes so integrated with the outer little self or human ego, that the dense substance of the physical body can no longer hold dominion. Through this integration, the body is purified by the Power of God within.

It is time for us to move into our Hearts. Transfiguration cannot occur on a mental level alone but must resonate through a selfless Heart. In that Inner Sanctuary Truth abides. The Truth is that a Master is one who has attained mastery over, not only the lower self, but *every* plane of being. Such mastery is attained through the Power of Love. Love is a magnet for Transfiguration. The greatest power in the Universe is Love. Love is Power, and Love is Wisdom. Love, Wisdom and

Power are inseparable. These qualities represent the TRINITY OF GOD and are anchored in every human Heart. Love is the cohesive essence which Unifies, yet gives complete Freedom. When applied to Transfiguration, it is ALWAYS Victorious.

This is the Cosmic Moment on Earth when matter will be Transfigured. The DNA in our cells is being reprogrammed by our God Self to accept higher sensory capabilites so that our physical vehicles will Ascend into the "Light Body." As this occurs, our forcefield of Divine Love will expand to engulf the entire planet Earth.

Visualization for a
Planetary Forcefield of Unconditional Love

Visualize: A magnetic Forcefield of Divine Love enfolding Planet Earth, attracting the Energy, Vibration and Consciousness of Universal Divine Love into our Cause of Planetary Transformation. Visualize Seven Mighty Solar Seraphim of Divine Love sustaining this Planetary Forcefield (at the four Cardinal Points around the Planet, as well as above, below and within the Earth). See and feel Humanity's Consciousness Uniting as One with this Forcefield, causing a global Activity of Healing through Love.

As you hold this visualization in your mind's eye, do the following rhythmic breath three times.

Breathing Statement:
(Inbreathing slowly) "I AM" Inbreathing the Healing Power of Unconditional Love into Humanity's Global Consciousness.
(Holding the Breath in) "I AM" Absorbing the Healing Power of Unconditional Love into Humanity's Global Consciousness.
(Exhaling slowly) "I AM" Expanding the Healing Power of Unconditional Love into Humanity's Global Consciousness.
(Holding the Breath out) "I AM" Projecting the Healing Power of Unconditional Love into Humanity's Global Consciousness.
(Repeat three times)

Our Forcefield of Unconditional Love, created through the Unified efforts of the Lightworkers on the Planet, is far more powerful in its impact on Humanity's global consciousness than any other forcefield of humanly generated energy which yet perpetuates the serious problems facing the Planet. **It is a Universal Law that, if the inner conditions or forces within Humanity's global consciousness are transformed through Love, the outer conditions of the world will proceed to reflect the Divine Plan for the Earth.**

The Divine Plan for the Earth is a living, active, all powerful forcefield that will produce Perfection if not interfered with through lower human free will. In the Heavenly Realms, the Beings of Light work purely and precisely with the great Forces of Cause knowing full well that the effects will take care of themselves. Most of us are currently trying to manage "effects" in our Lives rather than focusing on the "cause," which will truly change the situation from within.

To ensure the transformation of inner conditions, together we must create a Forcefield of Divine Love. Centered within Unity Consciousness, our collective Spiritual ability will enable each of us to accomplish this Divine Plan.

The Electronic Pattern for this Forcefield is a Magnetic Heart of Pure Divine Love enfolding Planet Earth. This Heart, formed through our Unified Consciousness, magnetically attracts the Energy, Vibration and Consciousness from every Ascended level of Being in this Universe into our Planetary Cause of manifesting the New Age of Spiritual Freedom that is now dawning.

There are Seven magnificent, radiant Solar Seraphim of Pure Divine Love Who have taken Their strategic positions around this Planet to assist us in this activity of Light. The Beings of Divine Love are stationed at the four Cardinal Points around the Earth, as well as above, below and directly within the center of the Planet. These Beings shall conduct a symphony of Love ensouling and interpenetrating our Beloved Earth. Each Lightworker on Earth is a power point of Light Unified in Consciousness with every other Lightworker, In-breathing, Absorbing, Expanding and Projecting this Forcefield throughout Humanity, the Nature and Elemental Kingdom, the Angelic Kingdom and the entire atmosphere of Earth. The God Presence within each Lightworker is the "open door" for this resplendent Light. The God Presence is the doer, the doing and the deed.

As we experience the manifestation of this Forcefield of Pure Divine Love, we see the deep colors of Love, smell the fragrance of Love and hear the Cosmic Tones and moving melodies of Love. Through this activity, we are truly Love in Action, collectively changing the core vibration of the primal Light Substance which has gone into all the present manifestations on Earth.

We are the *cause* of this magnetic Forcefield of Love anchored on Earth. Through this activity of Light, we are setting in place the basic Spiritual Forces of Divine Love over which Humanity will Ascend out of our long exile in darkness into the Realms of Light *permanently*.

As we Unify in Consciousness with the Kingdoms of Earth and the Realms of Heaven, we create an open door to explore and rediscover the greater Family of God in which we will find complete support for the fulfillment of our Divine Plan.

This is what the magnetic Forcefield of Divine Love will attract to each of us personally if we live within It. We will be raised into a profound re-awakening of Supreme Love Consciousness...to become again the Masters of Love we have always been and truly are here and now.

For the greatest success, we must feel ourselves as Beings of Love, being responsible for Loving this Sweet Earth and all Her Life Free.

AFFIRMATION OF DIVINE LOVE

I AM One with this Blessed Planet, and the Planet is One with me. The Seven radiant Seraphim of Light surround me in a Cosmic Forcefield of Divine Love-to the North, South, East and West of me--above me, below me and directly within the Divinity of my Heart...I AM now a Planetary Forcefield of Unconditional Love. The Love of God is now thriving on Earth through me. I feel the Heart of Love Healing the primal Light Substance of my four lower bodies and of all the physical, etheric, mental and emotional spheres of Earth. Together, with Humanity, I AM changing the inner conditions for the entire Planet, and I AM setting this Earth on a new Planetary course of Divine Love.

We must energize this Forcefield of Divine Love daily through the Holy Breath and meditation as we visualize the Cosmic Forcefield of the Heart of Love and the Seven Solar Seraphim of Divine Love. We must also feel complete Unity with *All* Life as we expand and project this Forcefield into every aspect of Humanity's day-to-day functioning, particularly any cause with which we have an affinity.

We accept that this Forcefield of Pure Divine Love is manifest now and forever through God's Holy Grace!

The cassette tapes to assist you in integrating this chapter into your daily life experience are listed on page 177.

CHAPTER
THREE

OWNER'S MANUAL FOR THE PHYSICAL BODY... ATTAINING ETERNAL YOUTH, VIBRANT HEALTH, RADIANT BEAUTY

The Body Elemental

When we first came into individualization and decided to enter the physical plane of experience, we were assigned two caretakers to assist us through our Earthly sojourn. One was from the Angelic Kingdom...a Guardian Angel, and one was from the Elemental Kingdom...a Body Elemental. The function of the Body Elemental is to supervise the building of the human form from conception through the gestation period. Then It monitors the four lower bodies as they grow and mature. It has agreed to stay with us until we have completed all of our lifetimes on Earth. The Body Elemental is actually the intelligence that is responsible for the function and well-being of our bodies.

In the beginning, when our Body Elemental volunteered to serve us throughout our Earthly adventure, It did so as an act of selfless service and Love. This intelligent Elemental Being was very aware of the beauty of our Holy Christ Self, and It knew that that Divine Presence was to be the master of the vehicles It would build. Our Body Elemental gave a solemn promise to obey the will of Humanity, believing, at the time, that our Holy Christ Self would always be in charge.

The Body Elemental vibrates, as does our Guardian Angel, at a frequency beyond our physical sight. Consequently, this Being is invisible, and we are usually oblivious to the service It provides us. But now, during this moment of opportunity, we must reacquaint ourselves with this selfless servant and make our peace with It.

When the human ego took command of our four lower bodies and began projecting into them all manner of putrification and decay, the Body Elemental was forced to outpicture gross mutations of disease, aging and death. This was certainly not what It had originally volunteered to do, but It was bound to the vow It had made to obey the will of Humanity. Initially, the Body Elemental continued to cooperate with the human ego hoping that the Holy Christ Self would regain rightful authority. After centuries of disappointment, It finally gave up, and the once Divine alliance between our Body Elemental and ourselves deteriorated into, first, antipathy, then hatred and finally open warfare. Instead of being our cooperative ally, our Body Elemental became our avowed enemy, never missing an opportunity to cause us distress or pain. This anger and resentment spread to the rest of the Elemental Kingdom: the fire, water, air and earth. The Elementals rebelled, declaring war against Humanity, and we have since experienced the volatile results of hurricanes, tornadoes, earthquakes, volcanic eruptions, plagues, pestilence, floods, famines, droughts, disease and on ad infinitum.

Since the Baptism of Divine Love that took place during the first Earth Summit, the majority of the Elemental Kingdom, *including our Body Elemental,* have agreed to Trust our promise to surrender our human ego and to give dominion of our bodies and the Earth back to our Holy Christ Self.

Some of the Elemental Kingdom is still distrusting and rebelling angrily against us, as we can witness by observing the destructive forces of nature acting out at the present time. We must be consistent in projecting our love and forgiveness into all aspects of the Elementals to calm these rebellious forces. The most powerful place we can begin is with our own Body Elemental. Remember, this Being volunteered to be with us in each and every embodiment, sustaining radiant bodies of perfection through which we could experience the physical plane. Instead, we forced it to create distorted, diseased, disfigured, bodies of pain and suffering. Now, we must convince this Elemental Being that we are truly sorry, and we are ready to cooperate with It and obey the Divine Laws of Vibrant Health. We must reach up in consciousness and tap the Realms of Truth for guidance, and we must seek out the most perfect, effective substances to heal and rejuvenate our bodies at an atomic cellular level.

The following information is pouring forth now to remind us of what we have forgotten. Read it with an open mind and an open Heart. Ask the Presence of God and the Body Elemental within you to confirm the Truth of this Sacred Knowledge.

Nourishing the Body Temple

Now that our Holy Christ Self has been united once again to the atomic cellular structures of our four lower bodies and the intelligent lifeforms within all physical matter, the Elementals, have agreed to work with us in loving cooperation, we are at long last in a position to restore our bodies to their original Divine Intent. In the beginning, our bodies were designed to reflect only the perfection of our Holy Christ Self. That reflection vibrates solely with the frequencies of *Eternal Youth, Vibrant Health and Radiant Beauty*. Every electron of our physical body is anxiously awaiting the opportunity to return to the Divine pattern it was created to outpicture, and that opportunity is being presented to each of us during this unique Cosmic Moment.

As we relinquish the grip our lower human ego has had on our bodies and reach up in consciousness into the enlightened mind of our Holy Christ Self, we will tap the wisdom and understanding that will allow us to rejuvenate our bodies at an accelerated pace. Remember, we have been told our transformation will take place "in the twinkling of an eye." That doesn't mean someone will wave a magic wand. It means we will learn to revere our bodies as the "Temple of the Most High Living God," and we will treat them with the utmost love and respect. We will evaluate the Divine Truth being revealed to us now, and we will apply it to our everyday lives according to our Heart's call. As this Sacred Knowledge is integrated into our daily behavior patterns, we will be lifted up and filled with the joy and happiness of not only our Holy Christ Self but the entire Company of Heaven, those selfless Beings of Light who have been patiently assisting us from inner levels and enthusiastically working to hasten our *awakening*.

Our human ego is an inversion of the Law. It has operated strictly to gratify our physical senses and has manipulated us into addictive, compulsive behavior patterns that couldn't possibly be further from the Truth of what we should be doing to sustain Vibrant Health, Eternal Youth and Radiant Beauty. Consequently, when we begin to learn what we need to do to promote perfection in our bodies, it seems rather extreme. We feel a little overwhelmed and sometimes even resentful. Usually a sense of resistance wells up in us, and we start to rebel. I want to assure you that those feelings are simply the temper tantrum of the human ego. This wayward aspect of our consciousness is fighting in any way it can to prevent us from taking its power away. We must recognize these feelings for what they are and deliberately command the human ego into the Light by stating:

Human ego, I Love you! I appreciate any learning experiences you have provided for me during my Earthly sojourn, but now it is time for my true God Reality, my Holy Christ Self, to have full dominion of my physical, etheric, mental and emotional bodies. Through the power of God "I AM", I command you into the Light and I Love you free!!!

Every time a thought of anger, resistance, fear or doubt pops into your mind, repeat the preceding decree. Then invoke your Holy Christ Self to take command of your four lower bodies with the following decree:

Through the Power of God anchored in every human Heart, I invoke my Holy Christ Self to take full command of my four lower bodies. Blessed One, walk through me and reflect through my thoughts, words, actions and feelings the perfection of Heaven. Remove any trace of resistance or discomfort, and allow me to apply the Laws of Vibrant Health, Eternal Youth and Radiant Beauty easily and effortlessly. I accept that with every breath I take "I AM" emulating the perfection of the Christ grown to full stature and now made manifest in the world of form.
So be it! "I AM"!

The Universal Laws of
Eternal Youth, Vibrant Health and Radiant Beauty

I would like you to read this information with an open mind and an open Heart, but I don't want you to ever accept *anything* as Truth just because somebody told you it was so. I want you to allow these words to resonate in your Heart, and as they do, ask your Holy Christ Self to reveal to you if these Laws apply to you.

These Laws have been taught in Mystery Schools for millennia. Now, because of the awakening and the Healing that has taken place, the masses of Humanity are finally in a position to learn these Laws. Each of us will respond to them in our own individual way. For some, it will be a very slow, gradual processs for others the Laws will be a welcome blessing, and they will be eagerly adapted into daily routines.

It is important for each of us to truly listen to our inner guidance and not try to force things we are not ready for. We need to be patient with ourselves and not beat ourselves up for what we perceive to be a lack of will power or a weak character defect. Our human ego has dominated us for lifetimes, and it is not going to give up easily. Consistency and perseverance are the keys to permanent changes in our behavior patterns. The more we invoke our Holy Christ Self, the easier it will be. When our Divine Self is the master of our bodies, the clamoring of our physical appetites will cease. We will truly desire only that which promotes our highest good. So rest assured, when your Christ Self is in command, the struggling will be over. Your daily disciplines will be a joy, and you will no longer feel deprived.

Physical Transformation is a multidimensional activity of Light. It involves what we put into our bodies in the way of food and drink, and it also involves what is projected out of our bodies in the way of thoughts, words, actions and feelings. I would like to address first what we are putting into our bodies.

Our eating and drinking habits have become such a source of entertainment and socializing that we have practically forgotten why we eat and drink in the first place. At some obscure level, we know we are supposed to eat to nourish our physical body, but from the foods we usually stuff in our faces, we obviously aren't too concerned if we give our body the correct nourishment or not. We wouldn't think of defiling our animals or our cars or any other machine with the atrocities we force our body to assimilate as it searches for a molecule of nutrition that it might actually be able to use to rebuild itself. Yet, this Temple of the Most High Living God is contaminated with putrification daily. It is time for us to become more aware and time for us to listen to our inner directives.

What we eat and what we drink has far more to do with our Spiritual growth or lack of Spiritual growth than we ever imagined. We've all heard the expression "It's what comes out of our mouths, not what goes into our mouths that makes the difference." Well, what comes out of our mouths is certainly important, but so is what goes into our mouths. Everything has energy and vibration associated with it, and our body absorbs the energy and vibration of everything we consume. If the food we eat is healthy and vibrantly alive, it regenerates our body. If it is devitalized and dead, it creates a vibration of death in our body that destroys the cells and breaks down the entire system. Because the body is such a miraculous instrument, it can fight off the vibration of death for awhile, but after the age of about 25, it gets weaker and weaker. We then begin to experience what we call aging, which is the gradual death of the body. After the age of 70 or 80, the body loses the ability to fight, and it finally dies.

We have been killing our physical body in this way for so long that we actually believe aging and death, as we experience it, is normal. Well, that couldn't be more inaccurate. Aging and death, as we know it, is a creation of the human ego and was never intended to be part of our Divine Plan. We need to let go of that obsolete belief and start anew.

Let's assume that we are coming to Earth for the first time, and this time our Holy Christ Self has given us an owner's manual for our physical bodies. This would include instructions on what we need to keep our bodies healthy.

Fuel for the Physical Body

The physical body requires a large variety of pure, *living* foods: Fruits, Vegetables, Sprouted Grains, Nuts and Seeds. (Notice it says a large *variety,* NOT a large *amount.*) If the foods you consume are fresh, clean, living (raw) foods, the body will be very well-nourished on small amounts. Raw foods contain not only the usual vitamins and minerals, but the *living life force* of the food, as well. This life force replenishes the vital *Light energy* that rejuvenates the body. It functions as a regenerator to energize the cells and organs of the body, thus maintaining youth, health and beauty.

In food that is cooked, frozen, processed or rotten, the life force has been destroyed. This can be easily seen with Kirlian photography. The raw food emits energy and light, the cooked food is dead and void of energy or light. When you consume dead food in any form, it registers as a vibration of death in the body. When you consume live food, it registers as life in the body. It's very simple: *live food promotes life; dead food promotes death*. That seems very logical, but if you evalute how much dead food the average person eats everyday, it's alarming. I could go into lots of detail about all of the things we shouldn't eat, but it's really quite obvious. *If it is dead--don't eat it*. Yes, I know, this means *all* devitalized, processed foods; cooked foods; flesh food or, as some people put it, don't eat anything that has a face. Don't drink drinks that are dead, which includes fermented alcoholic drinks or drinks that are filled with chemicals. That includes all alcoholic beverages, soft drinks, frozen drinks, and pasturized drinks. In other words, think LIFE!

Now, for some people, it's going to seem as though there is nothing left to eat, but that just isn't true. There are hundreds of wonderful living foods and delicious combinations you can create. It's true that you are going to have to be adventurous, but when you begin to see how much more alive, energetic, and youthful you feel, you'll love it.

Almost every fruit or vegetable on the market is delicious in its natural living state. Many times we've chosen, out of habit, to eat certain vegetables only if they're cooked, but we should experiment with everything and see how wonderful they are when eaten raw. Create light, healthy dressings out of raw oils and fresh herbs and spices. Combine different vegetables together for different tastes. All grains and legumes are very nutritious, but some are impossible to digest raw unless they are sprouted. Once they are sprouted, they are delicious in salads or just by themselves. They are a very good source of protein and minerals.

If you consume a large variety of healthily grown living foods, your body will normally have all the vitamins and minerals it needs for optimum health, but if you feel you may still want to take additional natural supplements, consult with a well-trained wholistic physician. When consuming healthy, living foods you will find that you are satisfied with very little food. The body is an intelligent organism, and it craves the vital life force of living food for survival. *When we eat dead food, our body continues craving the life force that has been destroyed, so we keep eating, but never feel satisfied.* That is the main reason for all of the obesity Humanity is experiencing. Ironically, half of the Planet is dieting and the other half is starving to death. If we had had our owner's manual when we came to Earth, neither obesity nor starvation would exist. A living foods diet is very easy and inexpensive. If that is what we had put our time and energy into, from the beginning, there would be a bountiful supply for everyone on Earth.

Wonder Foods

In addition to the abundance of fruits, vegetables, nuts, seeds and grains the Elemental Kingdom has provided for our sustenance, there are some potent, concentrated foods available that will nourish the cells of our bodies with the perfect balance of vitamins, minerals, amino acids and micro nutrients. These so called "wonder" foods enable us to eat much smaller amounts of food. They fill in the gaps of depleted nutrition and infuse our cells with vibrant life force.

During this time of awakening, we will become more aware of the gifts of the Elemental Kingdom that are especially designed to restore our vehicles to their original perfection. Many illumined souls are tapping the Sacred Knowledge in the Mind of God and discovering how to blend these concentrated substances into "Living Elixirs."

The "wonder" foods listed here are some of the tried and true substances, but every day new items are appearing on the market. It is important that we use our inner guidance and Divine discerning intelligence to be sure we are consuming what is right for our unique body. No two people are alike, and what is right for one person may not be right for someone else. I recommend that you experiment with one product at a time. Communicate with your Body Elemental. Ask your body to reveal to you if this product is enhancing the rejuvenation of your cells and organs. Pay close attention to how you feel and how your body reacts to the product. It's time we reunite with our Body Elemental and be in tune with how It is responding to the food and drink we consume. Our Body Elemental desperately wants us to return to the perfect body It originally agreed to sustain for us. If we will put forth the effort and let It know we are very sincere in our desire to restore our body to Vibrant Health, Eternal Youth and Radiant Beauty, It will joyously cooperate with us. But *we cannot be giving lip service to that fact while we continue to putrify our bodies with all manner of death and corruption.* Think deeply about this. Meditate on it, and invoke the full power of your Holy Christ Self to give you the strength and courage you need to succeed.

Blue Green Algae

Blue Green Algae is one of the most concentrated sources

of stored Light available on the Planet. Light is stored in plants in the chlorophyll through the process of photosynthesis, and Blue Green Algae has an accelerated capacity for chlorophyll production.

During this unique opportunity we are being given on Earth, the most important thing we can do is increase our cellular capacity to assimilate Light. All Transfiguration results from increasing the Light in every electron of our body. This has the effect of increasing our energy, vibration and consciousness.

In addition to its unique ability to store Light, Blue Green Algae is a whole living food that nourishes cells at a deep cleansing level. Blue Green Algae is a perfectly balanced life generating food that is especially rich in vitamins, enzymes, trace minerals, all essential amino acids, neuropeptides and chlorophyll.

If we will consume it daily, our cells will be efficiently nourished, thus promoting their perfect function and vibrant health.

There are many distributors for Blue Green Algae, but I would like to share with you the name of a source in case you don't have access to a distributor. These are people I trust, and I can assure you they will serve you with integrity and love. You may write them for detailed information on Blue Green Algae and other associated products.

Mr. and Mrs. Peter McGeoghegan
675 Fairview Drive, Suite 246
Carson City, NV 89701

Bee Pollen

Bee Pollen is one of nature's most perfect foods. It is gathered by bees from the part of the flower that contains the most concentrated essence of *life force*. Chemical analysis reveals that Bee Pollen contains virtually all known essential nutrients. The nutrients occur in a readily assimilable form that greatly promotes perfect biological health of the body.

Bee Pollen is easily obtainable in Health Food Stores.

Pure Water

It's hard to believe that pure water is considered a wonder food, but during this special time it is. Water is a conductor of Light, and it is imperative that we increase the amount of pure water we are consuming. We can add chlorophyll to it if we want to, and it will increase our ability to absorb Light. We can also charge the water we drink and bathe in with Light by using color crystals and Sacred Fire. Simply invoke the Divine Quality you want to charge into the water, and visualize the corresponding color and Sacred Fire blazing into the water. A crystal of the appropriate color placed in the water will amplify the Light you are invoking.

Sunlight

Sunlight is empowered with the Twelve-fold Solar Aspect of Deity, and it is critical to our survival on Earth. We need to be exposed daily, for a short period of time, to the full spectrum radiance of the Sun. The more bare skin it can shine on, the better. Sunlight increases our energy level and enables the electrons of our body to absorb more Divine Light.

Holy Breath

The sacred substance of Prana or Holy Breath is filled with the life force of Divine Energy and Light. We cannot survive for more than a few minutes without the Holy Breath. Deep breathing fills our cells with oxygen and life force and promotes vibrant health as it detoxifies and cleanses our cells.

Exercise

Exercise increases the circulation of precious nutrients, pure water and oxygen into our cells and organs. It strengthens every bodily function and enhances our feeling of well-being. Exercise should be part of our daily health routine. Thirty to forty minues of aerobic exercise daily will ensure a feeling of vitality and increase the proper elimination of the toxins in our bloodstream so our cells can easily assimilate the health producing nutrients we are consuming.

Transformational Programs

There are many programs appearing on the market that claim all kinds of miracles. I have experimented with several of them, and I would like to share with you information on a couple of them that I felt were outstanding. These two programs are very compatible, and in my experience, actually enhance each other. Their producers are genuinely interested in improving the quality of life for the Planet, and they are charging fair prices and operating from a high level of integrity.

The first program is called "The Human Ecology Program." It was developed by Raphael Ornstein, M.D. (also knows as Da Vid), founder of the San Francisco Medical Research Foundation. This program is a comprehensive health maintenance and rejuvenation process. It is designed to promote health through diet and detoxification. There are several biological keys to achieving vibrant health, and this program addresses all of them:

1. Markedly increasing the oxygen capacity of the blood.
2. Reducing and preventing the build-up of toxic free-radicals in our body.
3. Strengthening the neuroendocrine and immune systems of the body.

4.   Cleansing and detoxifying the blood, lymph and colon.
   You may obtain detailed information on the Human Ecology Program by writing to:

The San Francisco Medical Research Foundation
20 Sunnyside Avenue, Suite A-156
Mill Valley, CA 94941

Life Force

The second program I would like to tell you about includes a Body Balancing Elixir and a colon purification and detoxification process.

Life Force has several products that are especially designed to regenerate and rejuvenate the cells of the body and cleanse the colon so that the nutrition we consume will be assimilated properly.

Colon health is critical to the process of Transfiguration. From the time we are small, matter accumulates in our intestinal tract and putrifies, releasing toxins into the bloodstream that break down the body's natural regeneration process.   By cleansing the colon and removing the toxins, the assimilation of nutrients is greatly improved and the regeneration of healthy cells restored.

The Body Balance elixir contains the healing properties found in natural organic vitamins, macrominerals, trace minerals, amino acids and enzymes from both land and sea. It contains the extracts of healing plants grown on the land and harvested from the sea and used through the ages by healers of every nation.

For detailed information on the Life Force program you may write to:

Catherine and Bob Saltzman
1443 Adelsas Avenue
Encinitas, CA 92024

Colon Cleanse

There are many ways to cleanse the colon. It will be well worth your while to investigate the various options available. The colon therapist at our clinic will be happy to send you information or give you a free consultation if you are interested. Just contact:

Ron Chandler
Swan Clinic of Natural Healing
1001 North Swan Road
Tucson, AZ 85711 602/323-7133

In addition to eating vibrant living foods, cleansing our colon and detoxifying our bodies, drinking pure water, exercising and getting plenty of fresh air and Sunshine, we need to bless our bodies with cleanliness and reverence. Remember, this is an intelligent organism. Every meal and every drink should be consumed as a sacred repast, a sacrament. Chew each bite well, and with deep gratitude, ask your Body Elemental to absorb only that which will promote perfect health and rejuvenation in every cell and organ of your body. Monitor yourself, and eat only to the point of being satisfied. Don't overeat. Feel the life force coursing through your veins, replenishing and revitalizing every cell. Feel the joy of your Body Elemental as It is finally given permission by you to follow Its true Master, the Holy Christ Self, instead of the recalcitrant human ego.

There are thousands of good books on nutrition, but I think if I just list five that are most in alignment with the information pouring forth from the Realms of Illumined Truth, you will be more likely to read them.

1. Number one *must* reading is Gabriel Cousens', M.D., new book, *Conscious Eating,* published by Vision Books International, 510 Fifth Street, Santa Rosa, CA 95401.
2. *The Essene Gospel of Peace*, Book 1, by Edmund Bordeaux Szekely.
3. *The Human Ecology Program,* The San Francisco Medical Research Foundation, 20 Sunnyside Avenue, Suite A-156, Mill Valley, CA 94941.
4. *Ageless Aging,* by Leslie Kenton, published by Arrow Books Limited, 20 Vauxhall Bridge Road, London, England SWIV 25A.
5. *Raw Energy*, by Leslie and Susannah Kenton, published by Arrow Books Limited, 20 Vauxhall Bridge Road, London, England SWIV 25A.

FOOD FOR THOUGHT ON THE SUBJECT OF PHYSICAL TRANSITION

Death and Dying

As we begin to realize that Limitless Physical Perfection is, in fact, becoming a reality, there are several questions that arise in our minds. People often ask me, "Does this mean we are going to live on Earth forever?" The answer to that is no. The Earth is a schoolroom of learning, and we have come here to learn to become masters of energy, vibration and consciousness. When we complete our lessons here we will progress on into higher dimensions of learning on our return journey back to the Heart of our Father-Mother God.

In Richard Bach's book *Illusions,* he has a test to determine if our work on Earth is finished or not. The test is: if you are alive, it isn't.

What Limitless Physical Perfection does mean is that we will be living much longer, and we won't be dying just because our body has been so defiled by us that it can't live anymore. Instead we will live vibrant, healthy lives until our learning experiences for that particular lifetime are complete, then we will lay our body down, withdrawing our life force, and move into the next octave of learning. One day we won't even have to lay our body down and leave it behind. We will eventually take our body with us into the Light through the process of Ascension. That is probably going to be possible much sooner than we think.

Suicide

Another question that comes up when we're talking about death and dying is suicide. I am a counselor at a natural healing clinic, and often patients, enveloped in depression and hopelessness, will talk about contemplating suicide. Of course, in that moment, it is not enough to tell them we are never given anything we can't handle, even though that is the Truth. They are so buried in negativity that, from their perspective, it really does look like more than they can handle. It doesn't even help to assure them that if every single person that had ever committed suicide had stayed in their body, they would have proven that they were able to survive the challenge they were going through.

The reality is that when people think of suicide, all they think about is making the pain stop. They don't usually think about what is going to happen to them after they "die." They just want out of their present situation.

Because this comes up so often in my counseling, I have spent a great deal of time reaching into the Realms of Truth to research what happens to souls who have committed suicide. What I have been clearly shown is that suicide is the only way we leave the physical realm prematurely. Any other way we make our transition is part of the learning experience we have agreed to go through, regardless of how accidental the death appears. As we learn to effectively apply the Laws of Limitless Physical Perfection, our time of demise will be altered, and we will eliminate terminal diseases and aging, but even those changes are part of the plan.

As soon as a person commits suicide s/he is shown the panorama of the life just ended. We don't even lose consciousness when we die. In the panorama s/he is shown his/her life up to the moment of suicide and also the opportunites s/he was supposed to experience on Earth for the remainder of the life that s/he has now interrupted. Immediately, the soul recognizes what a terrible mistake s/he made. Our progress is always contingent on how we complete the experiences we have agreed to go through. If we don't successfully walk through our Earthly challenges, we cannot move to the next octave of

Learning. Therefore, a soul that has committed suicide recognizes instantly that they must now finish at inner levels what they had agreed to experience on Earth. We are multidimensional beings, and as soon as the soul recognizes the mistake, s/he is given the opportunity to move into another dimension where s/he recreates through his/her thoughts and feelings the *identical experience* s/he was going through on Earth. The problem now is that s/he doesn't have a physical body, so s/he doesn't have the peace of sleep. All of the anguish and despair s/he was experiencing on Earth is now present 24 hours a day. The only difference is that s/he has a greater level of awareness, so s/he knows there are no easy outs, and s/he understands s/he has no option but to progress through the experience.

At the time s/he was originally scheduled to "die," s/he completes this inner dimensional experience. In that moment s/he is given permission to proceed into the next Heavenly School of Learning. If a person was originally to be on Earth until s/he was 60 years old and commits suicide at the age of 40 years, then this inner level experience is created for 20 years.

I'm not sharing this information to make anyone feel bad, but rather to encourage us to walk through our challenges with determination and courage. When people are really desperate, usually all I have to say to them is imagine going through this pain without the peace of being able to go to sleep for a few hours everyday. For most depressed people, their only respite from the misery is when they are sleeping. The thought of not being able to sleep seems unbearable, and it works as a powerful deterrent.

Abortion

Another question clamoring for resolution is the issue of abortion. There are so many opinions and judgments being made over this situation that even those people trying to stop abortion are just adding to the problem. What we need to do is enter our Hearts and invoke the Sacred Fire of Truth and Compassion. When we are enveloped in this Divine Substance, we will be able to reach up in consciousness and perceive our Divine Plan in this matter.

The Truth is that we are not going to be able to legislate the elimination of abortion. What we must do is raise our consciousness and become more in tune with our Divine Plan on Earth. Unwanted pregnancies are a result of the ignorance of our lower human ego. As we've talked about before, this wayward aspect of our personality operates out of the need to gratify our physical senses, and it is totally out of touch with our Holy Christ Self.

As you can imagine, being born on Earth is a major event in our lives. It involves a very elaborate process *prior to conception,* and **no one sneaks into this physical plane by accident!!!** Once a soul has completed all of the necessary initiations at inner levels and is finally granted permission to embody on Earth, s/he is drawn before the Karmic Board, and the prospective parents are chosen. The Holy Christ Self of both the father and mother are then summoned before the Karmic Board and asked if they will accept responsibility for allowing this soul entrance into the physical plane of Earth, so that the soul can continue his/her learning process. Only after an affirmative agreement has been made by the father, mother and the soul, is conception allowed.

Now, because the conscious mind of the human ego is unaware of the agreement, when the parents or parent realize they have conceived, it is often a shock. The challenge of having the baby may seem overwhelming, and sometimes the only option seems like abortion. There is no such thing as death, so we don't "kill the baby," but what we do is deprive it of the vehicle it was going to use to experience the Earth plane. It may be hundreds of years before the exact right circumstances present themselves again for that particular soul's learning experience. That is a terrible setback for the soul and a tragedy for all concerned.

When we are reunited with our Holy Christ Self, this tragedy will cease. For one thing, we will be in tune enough with our Body Elemental and our Divine Plan that we won't be agreeing to allow a soul to come through us unless we consciously know that we are going to be able to handle it. We will understand that if we become pregnant, it is a learning experience that our Higher Self has agreed at some level to go through. This is true, whether we are talking about a loving conception or even rape or incest. Negative experiences are karmic liabilities that we have agreed at some level to transmute. They are lessons that we have agreed to experience to accelerate our growth.

If the fetus is deformed or defective mentally, that is also a learning experience that all involved have agreed at inner levels to go through. Aborting a deformed fetus does not mean the soul won't need to experience that lesson; it just means it is delayed until other parents are found that will allow the soul to be born with the physical or mental challenge.

It is obvious that the only way the problem of abortion is going to be alleviated is for *all* Humanity to become One with their Holy Christ Self. Until that happens, the human ego, functioning out of fear, will perpetuate abortion.

In my experience, I think the majority of people don't really approve of abortion, but they feel if women are determined to have them, then they at least want them to be safe. They don't want little thirteen year-old girls in the alley with a coat hanger. Most people really have a pro-life *and* a pro-choice attitude.

Instead of condemning, judging and criticizing people who are making their choices the best they can, according to their wisdom and their understanding, we need to invoke the Law of Forgiveness for them and ask their Holy Christ Selves to guide them into the Realms of Illumined Truth.

What to do About the Designer Diseases
We Have Created

It is interesting to note that as we "ingeniously" develop more lethal pollutants in the form of pesticides, preservatives, antibiotics, drugs, synthetic dead foods, devitalized processed foods, toxic chemical additives, etc., our bodies are simultaneously manifesting "designer" diseases such as AIDS, chronic fatigue syndrome, Legionnaires' disease, candida and a multitude of other maladies that attack the various systems and organs of the body. It is glaringly evident that in areas of the world that have not been contaminated with our so called modern diet, the afflictions plaguing Western society are virtually unheard of.

Our body is a miraculous organism that was originally designed to be self-healing. It has incomparable methods of purification and detoxification. The body's elimination system is truly magnificent, and the immune system is mind boggling in its effectiveness. Every single day it fights off every conceivable form of virus, bacteria, germ, infection, disease and malfunction. As long as the systems of the body are allowed to function in the manner that they were originally created to function, we have the ability to sustain vibrant health. What has happened, unfortunately, is that through the development of our civilized world, we have been so focused on developing food products that are "bigger," "better," "faster," "cheaper," "newer," "prettier," "more convenient," "more profitable," "sweeter," "saltier," "crunchier," "longer shelf life," etc., we have forgotten that we eat to maintain health in our body. We have putrified our bodies with such a conglomeration of toxins that all of our systems are overloaded and unable to efficiently rid the body of the contaminants that break down the immune system and allow disease to take hold of the cells and organs.

Defiling our bodies with devitalized food and toxins is not the only way we are manifesting designer diseases. We have also created an unprecedented society of stress, anxiety, fear, corruption and negativity. This results in negative thinking and emotional chaos. All of these factors further exacerbate the breakdown of the body and the demise of our body's immune system and other health maintaining systems. The peculiar maladies appearing on the screen of life are actually a desperate SOS from our bodies. It is critical that we heed these warnings and start paying attention to the atrocities we are perpetrating on our bodies. Fortunately, since our bodies are such incredible instruments, they have an unbelievable capacity to restore themselves if we will only stop bombarding them with self-destructive foods, drinks, thoughts, feelings and actions.

It is not nearly as difficult as it may seem to turn around our downward spiral into disease and death. We need to *wake up* and listen to what our body is crying out for. We need to return to simplicity in our eating habits and restore our behavior patterns to constructive thinking and harmonious emotions. There is an expression that "The price of Freedom is eternal vigilance." It is imperative that we become cognizant of what we are consuming in the way of food and drink and what we are allowing our attention to focus on in the way of thoughts and feelings.

In 1977, a Nobel Prize was granted in the field of medicine for research done in the mental aspects of healing. It was discovered that joy and happiness, as well as laughter, cause electrical impulses in the brain that release hormones that enhance our natural immune system. Conversely, anger, resentment and hatred cause the release of hormones that suppress our natural immune system. It has also been found that tears from laughter, tears from grief and tears from peeling onions have entirely different chemical compositions.

The incredibly exciting part of our greater awareness is that even though, through a lack of understanding, we may have done things in the past that attributed to the current state of *"dis-ease"* in our physical body, we now have the practical tools available to help us correct the situation. The importance of understanding our responsibility in the breakdown of our natural immune system is certainly not to instill blame or guilt, but rather to help us understand that disease is mostly a human creation, and therefore, we as human beings have the power to do something about it.

I would like to share with you now some information that will help you apply the natural resources available to all of us that will accelerate the healing process. This information is *not* intended to take the place of sound medical assistance, but it can easily be incorporated with any treatment you are presently taking.

To begin our journey back to vibrant health and vitality, we must expand our self-awareness.

At the present time, the medical world is declaring as much as 80 percent of all illness to be psychosomatic. Many people think this means the illness is all in the head or imaginary, but that is not what psychosomatic means at all. A psychosomatic illness is a bodily disorder or malfunction that is *induced by mental or emotional disturbances*. This does not mean it is all imagination, but rather it is a physical illness that has been created through the misuse of thoughts and feelings.

This is a very complicated subject, and we have truly just begun to scratch the surface of discovering the effects of our thoughts and feelings on the health of our physical body, but we seem to be proving more and more that "As a man thinketh in his Heart, so he is." What we hold in our consciousness, we begin to manifest in our physical body. In my field of counseling, I work specifically with helping people accept responsibility in the healing process of their bodies. Far too many times I have seen the symptoms of an illness subside with medical treatment only to recur a short time later. We can treat symptoms forever and temporarily achieve a semblance of relief, but if we don't correct whatever it is that caused the malfunction of our immune system and allowed the illness to take hold of our bodies, it will continue to recur. To attain vibrant health, it is imperative that we evaluate our illness and try to discover just why our physical bodies became susceptible to disease.

Each of us individually is responsible for the health of our body, and only we can accurately determine what has occurred in our lives that affected us so intensely that we allowed the breakdown of our physical body as a result of it. In most instances, this is certainly not a deliberate or a conscious decision on our part, but it is the end result.

As a counselor, it is not my job to tell people what they are doing wrong, but merely to function as a catalyst in helping them to the point of realization through their own self-awareness.

My patients and I together have discovered many very interesting things about the manifestation of disease. This may seem like an oversimplification, and I am in no way suggesting that this is true in every case, but many times we have observed that the malfunction of the physical body is due to years of persistent negative attitudes, fears, prejudices and beliefs. The possibilities of this occurrence are legion. I feel confident in saying the majority of diseases are caused by the misapplication of the law of harmony through negative patterns of thought, opinions, attitudes, beliefs and feelings. Through scientific research, we have discovered that when the sentiments of envy, hate, fear, anger and resentment are habitual emotions in the body, they are capable of starting organic changes that actually result in genuine disease. Scientists have stated that there is mind-power in every cell, and each cell is filled with life, Light, intelligence and substance which form our atomic structure. When we continually send destructive messages to the intelligence within these cells, they begin to obey our command and eventually outpicture our distorted programming.

In order to restore the physical body back into an instrument of vibrant health, we need to thoroughly evaluate our thinking patterns and attitudes. After we have pinpointed the problem, we can then take the necessary steps to change our destructive habits and begin drawing perfect health into every cell, organ and function of our bodies.

The first step in the healing process is to stop our destructive habits. We need to observe and monitor what is going on in our body and strive, through self-discipline, to eliminate negative habits that are self-defeating.

We need to apply *all* of the factors of good health if we are to attain a vibrant state of health. We may be physically supplying our body with the correct balance of nutrition, but if we are still bombarding it with negative thoughts, feelings or memories, our nutritional efforts will be to no avail. So, in addition to proper care of our physical body, we need to be cognizant and in control of our thoughts, words and actions. We must be deliberate about health. We know that whatever we put our attention and energy into we intensify. Therefore, it is critical for us to stop giving power to the disease through our fear and worry.

For instance, we think of cancer as a powerful entity that comes in and ravages our body. Actually, cancer cells are very weak, confused cells and can *only* take hold of our body when we are in a low state of immunity. We need to put our attention on what we want, not what we don't want. Through creative visualization we need to begin seeing, feeling and thinking of ourselves in a state of vibrant health.

It is important to continue with sound medical treatment throughout the healing process whenever it is indicated, but don't allow anyone to instill a feeling of hopelessness in you.

Resentment, anger, fear, hatred and all of the other negative emotions we may feel toward the disease only compound the problem. Disease is a form of misqualified energy, and there is no way to destroy negative energy. All we can do is raise it back into a harmonious frequency of vibration, actually love it free. So instead of hating our disease, we need to work with it just like we do any other negative circumstance that is occurring in our life. We need to acknowledge that this is our own energy we misqualified at one time or another during our sojourn on Earth. We should then be grateful for the opportunity to transmute this energy back to its original perfection, and ask for forgiveness for misqualifying this precious gift of life. Finally, we should fill the energy with the pink essence of pure love and literally love it free.

1. *Acceptance* - Acknowledging it is our own misqualified energy.
2. *Gratitude* - For the opportunity to transmute the vibration of this misqualified energy back to its original perfection.
3. *Forgiveness* - For abusing our precious gift of life.
4. *Love* - Loving the misqualified energy back to a state of harmony.

These are catalysts in the healing process. After applying the four steps, we can accelerate the healing process by consciously accepting, through the efficacy of faith, our ability to use the full power of our mind to heal. Then reinforce this faith with positive affirmations, creative visualization, deliberate channeling of healing energy into the body, controlled breathing exercises and the buoyant feeling of success.

Vegetarianism

The final thing I want to discuss in reference to death and dying is vegetarianism. There is a lot of discussion as to whether it is all right to eat fish and chicken, but just not eat red meat. Well, that all depends on why you have chosen a lifestyle of vegetarianism. What I am talking about in this book is raising the energy, vibration and consciousness of our four lower bodies. In order to do that, we need to consume foods filled with living life force. Animals of any kind, of course, must be killed in order for us to eat them, even if they are eaten raw. That always brings up the question of whether or not fruits and vegetables are "killed" when we eat them, and that is what I want to discuss here.

All that we consume is part of the Elemental Kingdom. Any Elemental that has evolved to the point of *locomotion* is no longer appropriate for human consumption. Elementals that walk, slither, fly or swim, in any form, are abiding *within* their Elemental body, just as you and I, who walk, abide in our Elemental (physical) body. If that body is killed, it interrupts the Elemental's opportunity to experience the physical plane, just as it does for us if someone kills our body. In killing an Elemental body of any kind, we have interfered with the progress of that being, and we have incurred a certain karmic liability.

When we consume Elemental substance that has not evolved to the point of locomotion, it is a very different situation. Stationary Elementals, which include all vegetables, fruits, nuts, seeds, grains, grasses and water *are the outpictured thoughtforms* of the Elemental Beings and do not house the Elemental itself. These thoughtforms are specifically created to nourish the physical bodies of mobile Human Beings and mobile Elementals. Everything that we could possibly need to sustain Limitless Physical Perfection has been provided for us through the thoughtforms of the Elemental Kingdom. We do not need to "kill" a single living thing to sustain our bodies on Earth. What we are now really understanding is that not only do we not need to kill anything, but it is a karmic liability if we do.

This is truly the dawn of the Permanent Golden Age. In this Age of Enlightenment, Humanity, Elementals and Angels will walk hand-in-hand in loving cooperation. It is time for us to *awaken* to that Truth and time for us to volunteer to be pioneers in proving the Laws of God's Will on Earth. These Divine Laws are the Laws of *Limitless Physical Perfection.*

The cassette tapes to assist you in integrating this chapter into your daily life experience are listed on page 177.

ADDITIONAL BOOK & AVAILABLE TAPES

THE AWAKENING...
ETERNAL YOUTH, VIBRANT HEALTH, RADIANT BEAUTY

by
Patricia Diane Cota-Robles

Aging, disease, deterioration and death as we know it were never part of the original Divine Plan on Earth. These miserable maladies are part of our human miscreation. They are the result of the "fall of man," a tragic time aeons ago when Humanity began experimenting with our creative faculties of thought and feeling in ways that were conflicting with God's Will. These distortions of our physical body have become such a common part of our everyday reality that we have accepted them as "normal." Actually nothing could be more abnormal.

Now, as we lift up in consciousness and tap the Realms of Illumined Truth, we are awakening within us the Truth of who we really are...Sons and Daughters of God, and we are realizing that the Divine Plan for Planet Earth and all Her life is Limitless Physical Perfection. This is not some far fetched dream, this is a very real opportunity.

Continued within the pages of this important, timely book is the Sacred Knowledge from the Realms of Truth that will enable each of us to Transform our bodies into ETERNAL YOUTH, VIBRANT HEALTH and RADIANT BEAUTY.

There is a set of tapes that coincides with this book that will assist you in assimilating this Truth.

See order form on the back of this page.

ORDER FORM
THE NEW AGE STUDY OF HUMANITY'S PURPOSE

THE AWAKENING...
ETERNAL YOUTH, VIBRANT HEALTH,
RADIANT BEAUTY

Book $12.95 + $2.00 P&H* _____

(for first book)
for each additional book $.75 P&H

THE AWAKENING...TAPES

1. THE TRANSFIGURATION OF OUR PHYSICAL BODY
$9.00 + $1.50 P&H _____

2. BECOMING YOUR HOLY CHRIST SELF
THE TRUE MEANING OF "THE SECOND COMING"
PART I & II (2 Tapes) $18.00 + $2.00 P&H _____

3. MORNING EXERCISES FOR PHYSICAL
TRANSFORMATION AND
EVENING EXERCISES FOR PHYSICAL TRANSFORMATION
(2 Tapes) $18.00 + $2.00 P&H _____

4. OWNER'S MANUAL FOR THE PHYSICAL BODY
ATTAINING ETERNAL YOUTH, VIBRANT HEALTH,
RADIANT BEAUTY $9.00 + $1.50 P&H _____

*Postage & Handling
Add $4.50 for Canada & Mexico
Add $8.00 for all other countries

BOOKS & TAPES SUBTOTAL _____

+ POSTAGE & HANDLING _____

TOTAL _____

Name _____

Address _____

City _____ State _____ Zip _____

Country _____ Telephone _____

Please send check or money order to The New Age Study of Humanity's Purpose, Inc.,
P.O. Box 41883, Tucson, AZ 85717 U.S.A. FAX # (602) 323-8252

WHEN PAYING BY VISA OR MASTER CARD, PLEASE FILL OUT
AND RETURN THIS COUPON

VISA ☐   MASTERCARD ☐

Amt. to be charged _____ Expiration on Card _____

Account Number _____

PRINT Name on Card _____

Signature _____

ADDITIONAL BOOK & AVAILABLE TAPES

TAKE CHARGE OF YOUR LIFE
by Patricia Diane Cota-Robles

There is an awakening taking place on this Planet, an increased awareness that is prompting people to search for solutions to the trials and tribulations of their daily lives.

Take Charge Of Your Life is elegant in its simplicity, clearly presented, and easy to understand. It is a unique and important book which presents concrete, practical step-by-step instructions that will give you specific tools and techniques necessary to ATTAIN YOUR FINANCIAL FREEDOM; CREATE WONDERFUL, LOVING RELATIONSHIPS; REACH YOUR OPTIMUM LEVEL OF SUCCESS AND EXCELLENCE: RESTORE YOUR BODY TO VIBRANT HEALTH: DEVELOP YOUR HIGHEST SPIRITUAL POTENTIAL; and TRULY BECOME THE MASTER OF YOUR LIFE *instead of the victim of your experiences.*

Take
Charge
of Your
Life

Patricia Diane Cota-Robles

$8.95   162 Pages

A series of tapes has been produced by Patricia Diane Cota-Robles to coincide with the book *TAKE CHARGE OF YOUR LIFE.* The tapes consist of a lesson, guided visualizations and mediations to help us utilize the tools presented in the book easily and effectively.

AVAILABLE TAPES FOR...
TAKE CHARGE OF YOUR LIFE
by
Patricia Diane Cota-Robles

A series of tapes has also been produced by Patricia Diane Cota-Robles to coincide with the book *TAKE CHARGE OF YOUR LIFE*. The tapes consist of a lesson, guided visualizations and meditations to help us utilize the tools presented in the book easily and effectively.

1. **YOU CAN TAKE CHARGE OF YOUR LIFE** **$9.00**
   The Key to Self-Mastery Is Self-Awareness–The Power of Thought–Monitoring Your Emotions–Creative Visualizations–Setting Goals

2. **UNCONDITIONAL LOVE** **$9.00**
   Transforming Your Relationships–The Power of Unconditional Love–Four Steps to Love Your Negative Energy FREE

3. **THE KEY TO FINANCIAL FREEDOM** **$9.00**
   Poverty Is NOT A Virtue–Clearing Your Relationships With Money–Money Is A Source of Energy...PERIOD–Opening Up to God's Limitless Flow of Abundance

4. **HEALING** **$9.00**
   Maintaining Health In Your Physical Bodies–Disease Is Often Self-Inflicted–Mental Aspects of Dis-ease and Healing–Visualization for Healing–Breathing Exercises

5. **MAGNETIZING PERFECTION INTO YOUR LIFE THROUGH THE CHAKRA CENTERS** **$9.00**
   Demystifying the Chakras–Chakras, Your Body's Electrical System–Cleansing and Balancing the Chakras–Using the Chakras As An Effective Tool to Harmonize Your Life

6. **HARMONY, COLOR AND MUSIC** **$9.00**
   The Use of Color and Music to Help You Reach Your Highest Potential–Color and Qualities of the Seven Spiritual Rays–Color Meditations–Music, A Sacred Science

7. **ALIGNING WITH YOUR DIVINE PURPOSE FOR "THE CAMPAIGN FOR THE EARTH"** **$9.00**
   Recognizing Our True God Reality–Eliminating Low Self-Esteem–Fulfilling Our Mission On Earth

8. **MEDITATIONS TO TRANSFORM YOUR LIFE** **$9.00**
   Guided Meditations, Visualizations and Affirmations to Help You Establish Positive Thinking Patterns and Transmute Old Belief Systems That No Longer Support Your Highest Good

9. **GETTING IN TOUCH WITH YOUR HIGHER SELF** **$9.00**
Communing With the God Presence Within–The Key to Spiritual Freedom–Entering the Realms of Illumined Truth–Perceiving Your Divine Plan

10. **THE WORLD HEALING MEDITATION AND PLANETARY TRANSFORMATION** **$9.00**
Balancing and Purifying Your Four Lower Bodies–Become the Clearest, Most Powerful Channel of Light You Can Possibly Be–Transforming the Earth Into FREEDOM'S HOLY STAR–Healing Planet Earth

The tapes in the *TAKE CHARGE OF YOUR LIFE* series are $9.00 each plus $1.50 postage and handling for each tape, or you may purchase the entire set of 10 tapes at a SPECIAL DISCOUNT RATE OF $75.00 plus $5.50 postage and handling–**A SAVINGS OF $15.00.**

To order see order form.

ORDER FORM
THE NEW AGE STUDY OF HUMANITY'S PURPOSE

Number of Copies

TAKE CHARGE OF YOUR LIFE
BOOK $8.95 + $2.00 P & H* _____
(for First Book)

.75 P & H
(for Each Additional Book)

TAKE CHARGE OF YOUR LIFE...TAPES

1. YOU CAN TAKE CHARGE OF YOUR LIFE
$9.00 + 1.50 P & H _____

2. UNCONDITIONAL LOVE
TRANSFORMATION
$9.00 + $1.50 P & H _____

3. THE KEY TO FINANCIAL FREEDOM
$9.00 + $1.50 P & H* _____

4. HEALING $9.00 + $1.50 P & H _____

5. MAGNETIZING PERFECTION INTO
YOUR LIFE THROUGH THE CHAKRA
CENTERS $9.00 + $1.50 P & H _____

6. HARMONY, COLOR AND MUSIC
$9.00 + $1.50 P & H _____

7. ALIGNING WITH YOUR DIVINE
PURPOSE FOR "THE CAMPAIGN
FOR THE EARTH"
$9.00 + $1.50 P & H _____

8. MEDITATIONS TO TRANSFORM
YOUR LIFE $9.00 + $1.50 P & H _____

9. GETTING IN TOUCH WITH YOUR
HIGHER SELF $9.00 + $1.50 P & H _____

10. WORLD HEALING MEDITATION–
PLANETARY TRANSFORMATION
$9.00 + $1.50 P & H _____

11. ENTIRE SET OF TAPES
$75.00 + $5.50 P & H* *(SAVE $15.00)* _____

BOOKS & TAPES SUBTOTAL _____
+ POSTAGE & HANDLING _____
TOTAL _____

*POSTAGE & HANDLING
Add $4.50 for Canada & Mexico
Add $8.00 for all other countries

(continued on other side)

NAME _____

ADDRESS _____

CITY _____ STATE _____ ZIP _____

COUNTRY _____ TELEPHONE _____

Please send check or money order for entire order to:
The New Age Study of Humanity's Purpose, Inc.
P.O. Box 41883, Tucson, Arizona 85717   U.S.A.
FAX # (602) 323-8252

WHEN PAYING BY VISA OR MASTERCARD, PLEASE FILL OUT AND RETURN THIS COUPON.

VISA ☐   MASTERCARD ☐

Amount to be charged _____

Account Number _____

Card Expires _____

PRINT Name on Card _____

Signature _____

THE NEXT STEP...
Re-unification with the Presence of God within Our Hearts

by
Patricia Diane Cota-Robles

Now, during this critical moment on Earth, we are being given unparalleled knowledge and wisdom that will enable each of us to re-unite with the part of our consciousness that ALWAYS aspires to the highest level of EXCELLENCE.

As the vibratory rate of the Planet increases, we are being lifted up closer to the realms of Illumined Truth in the Octaves of Perfection. This Realm pulsates with the knowledge and wisdom of the Ages. As this Illumination enters our consciousness, it provides us with very practical tangible tools and techniques that open the door for us to go within and tap the Power of our Divinity. When this occurs, our true God-Self bursts the bonds of human limitation and takes full dominion of our Lives.

Once we have re-united with our Higher Self–our God Presence "I AM"–It will guide us unerringly, as we create for ourselves Lives of JOY, HAPPINESS, ABUNDANCE, HEALTH, LOVE, FULFILLMENT, PURPOSE, SUCCESS and VICTORY.

This very timely book contains within its pages the Sacred Knowledge pouring forth from the Realms of TRUTH. As we apply this knowledge in our everyday Lives, we will experience a Transformation taking place. Our Lives will change. They will begin to reflect the Happiness, Harmony and Success we have been longing for. As we develop the simple skills taught in this significant book, we will experience more Loving relationships, Financial Freedom, Vibrant Health, Happiness, Fulfilling Careers, Spiritual Growth, Joyous Selfless Service, Inner Peace, Optimism and TOTAL SELF-MASTERY.

$14.98   369 Pages

"Know the TRUTH and the TRUTH shall set you FREE!"

The Next Step...

Re-unification with the Presence of God within our Hearts
Patricia Diane Cota-Robles

Patricia Diane Cota-Robles has also produced a series of tapes that coincide with the chapters of the book. The tapes will assist each person to absorb the maximum benefit from this Sacred Knowledge.

Each tape contains important information exercises, visualizations, affirmations, meditations and techniques that will set us FREE from our self-inflicted lack and limitation.

SPECIAL DISCOUNT–SAVE $25.00
by ordering the entire set of tapes.
$120.00 for all 16 tapes

THE NEXT STEP...

A. GOD'S WILL $9.00
The Will of God Is Perfection–Humanity's Fall From the Will of God–Exposing the World of Illusion in the Light of Reality–Humanity's Return Journey Back to the Will of God–Effectively Utilizing God's Will in Our Daily Lives.

B. THE WORLD HEALING MEDITATION AND PLANETARY TRANSFORMATION $9.00
This meditation tape cleanses our four lower bodies and prepares us to be the clearest possible channels of Healing Light–Visualization for the Transformation of Planet Earth into Freedom's Holy Star.

C. ENLIGHTENMENT $9.00
"Ye Are Gods"–In The Beginning..."I AM"–The Original Divine Plan–Earth's Return Journey Home

D. DIVINE LOVE $9.00
The Power of Divine Love–Love...And Let It Begin With Me–The Children of Love: Tolerance, Patience, Kindness, Humanitarianism, Reverence, Balance–Communication; The Key to Harmonious Relationships

E. PURITY $9.00
Purity is the Heart of Creation–The Miracle of Resurrection–Resurrecting The Divine Pattern Within–The Immaculate Concept–The Goal of Life Is the Ascension

F. TRUTH $9.00
The Empowerment of All God Qualities on Earth through the Supreme Initiation.

G. MINISTERING GRACE **$9.00**
Ministration is an activity of Grace–The Fourth Dimension is Established On Earth–The Opening of the Seventh and Final Angelic Vortex–Accepting the Power Within: Becoming the Divine Image Embodied in Flesh.

H. STAR★LINK 88 . . . . **$9.00**
This is a Powerful Activity of Light in which Humanity unites with the Angelic Kingdom to Assist this Sweet Earth as She Ascends into the Realms of Harmony and Balance.

**I. TRANSMUTING THE PAST THROUGH
THE POWER OF FORGIVENESS** **$9.00**
Utilizing the Power of Transmutation–The Violet Flame of Forgiveness and Freedom.

J. FREEDOM **$9.00**
Seven Steps to Precipitation: The Science of Succeeding in Your Purpose–Violet Flame Class

K. CLARITY **$9.00**
The Rebirth of our Planetary Identity into our God Identity–Through the Ray of Clarity, the Traps of the World of Illusion are Revealed

L. HARMONY **$9.00**
Harmony and Balance: The Path to our Eternal Freedom–The Twelve Universal Laws

M. ETERNAL PEACE **$9.00**
The Great Silence–Eternal Peace, The Open Door to Spiritual Freedom and Liberty

N. DIVINE PURPOSE **$9.00**
Happiness and Joy: Our Divine Birthright, Our Choice–Fulfilling Our Divine Purpose: A Step-By-Step Process

O. TRANSFORMATION **$9.00**
Transformation–Preparing for the Earth's Ascension into the Fourth Dimension

P. FROM HERE TO FOREVER **$11.00**
This tape contains wonderful songs sung by Peaches. Songs that lift the Soul and inspire the Consciousness

The tapes are $9.00 each (Peaches' tape is $11.00). plus $1.50 postage and handling per tape, or you may purchase THE ENTIRE SET OF 16 TAPES FOR A SPECIAL DISCOUNT RATE OF $120.00–**A SAVINGS OF $25.00.** Postage and handling for the complete tape package is $5.50.
To order see order form.

**The New Age Study of Humanity's Purpose
P.O. Box 41883
Tucson, Arizona 85717
FAX # (602) 323-8252**

ORDER FORM
THE NEW AGE STUDY OF HUMANITY'S PURPOSE

Number of Copies

THE NEXT STEP

BOOK $14.98 + $2.00 P & H*
(for First Book)

.75 P & H
(for Each Additional Book)

THE NEXT STEP...TAPES

A. GOD'S WILL $9.00 + 1.50 P & H

B. WORLD HEALING & PLANETARY
TRANSFORMATION
$9.00 + $1.50 P & H

C. ENLIGHTENMENT
$9.00 + $1.50 P & H

D. DIVINE LOVE $9.00 + $1.50 P & H

E. PURITY $9.00 + $1.50 P & H

F. TRUTH $9.00 + $1.50 P & H

G. MINISTERING GRACE
$9.00 + $1.50 P & H

H. STAR*LINK 88 $9.00 + $1.50 P & H

I. TRANSMUTING THE PAST
$9.00 + $1.50 P & H

J. FREEDOM $9.00 + $1.50 P & H

K. CLARITY $9.00 + $1.50 P & H

L. HARMONY $9.00 + $1.50 P & H

M. ETERNAL PEACE
$9.00 + $1.50 P & H

N. DIVINE PURPOSE
$9.00 + $1.50 P & H

O. TRANSFORMATION
$9.00 + $1.50 P & H

P. FROM HERE TO FOREVER
$11.00 + $1.50 P & H

Q. ENTIRE SET OF TAPES
$120.00 + $5.50 P & H* *(SAVE $25.00)*

SUBTOTAL BOOKS & TAPES _____

*POSTAGE & HANDLING   + POSTAGE & HANDLING _____
Add $4.50 for Canada & Mexico
Add $8.00 for all other countries   TOTAL _____

(continued on other side)

NAME _____

ADDRESS _____

CITY _____ STATE _____ ZIP _____

COUNTRY _____ TELEPHONE _____

Please send check or money order for entire order to:
The New Age Study of Humanity's Purpose, Inc.
P.O. Box 41883, Tucson, Arizona 85717   U.S.A.
FAX # (602) 323-8252

WHEN PAYING BY VISA OR MASTERCARD,
PLEASE FILL OUT AND RETURN THIS COUPON.

VISA   ☐   MASTERCARD   ☐

Amount to be charged _____

Account Number _____

Card Expires _____

PRINT Name on Card _____

Signature _____

ADDITIONAL BOOK & AVAILABLE TAPES

YOUR TIME IS AT HAND
by Patricia Diane Cota-Robles

You are a Son or Daughter of God and regardless of how far you may feel you are from being worthy of that honor, the Truth is you are a Child of God right here and right now. You have within you this very moment all of the potential, all of the knowledge, all of the skill and ability, you need to truly express that full Perfection blazing in your Heart. This informative book will give you the sacred tools to unlock your full Divine potential.

These are very confusing times and there is so much misinformation and disinformation about all of the things going on in our individual lives and on the Planet that we are feeling frustrated, anxious and overwhelmed. But, even in the midst of all of the chaos, we are on the brink of becoming our true God Reality.

232 Pages $11.00

This transformation is tangibly available to each and every one of us now, and it can be Victoriously accomplished. It is time for the struggling and misery to be over. It is time for us to co-create, with God, lives of Love, Prosperity, Happiness and Fulfillment.

This book will give you the tools you've been looking for. It will also give you greater Understanding and Hope.

AVAILABLE TAPES
YOUR TIME IS AT HAND
by
Patricia Diane Cota-Robles

A series has been produced by Patricia to coincide with the chapters in the book. The tapes will assist each person to absorb the maximum benefit from this Sacred Knowledge.

CHAPTER ONE...SET OF THREE TAPES
   YOU HAVE COME TO SAVE THE EARTH...
   AND YOUR TIME IS AT HAND
   PART I – PART II – PART III $25.00

CHAPTER TWO...SET OF TWO TAPES
   NOW IS THE OPPORTUNITY FOR LIMITLESS
   PHYSICAL PERFECTION
   PART I – PART II $18.00

CHAPTER FOUR...ONE TAPE
   THE GIFT TO RECLAIM YOUR PROSPERITY . . . $ 9.00

BOOK – YOUR TIME IS AT HAND $11.00

ORDER FORM
THE NEW AGE STUDY OF HUMANITY'S PURPOSE

Number of Copies

YOUR TIME IS AT HAND
BOOK $11.00 + $2.00 P & H* _____
(for First Book)
.75 P & H
(for Each Additional Book)

YOUR TIME IS AT HAND ... TAPES

1. **SET OF THREE TAPES**
   YOU HAVE COME TO SAVE THE EARTH ...
   AND YOUR TIME IS AT HAND
   PART I – PART II – PART III
   $25.00 + $2.00 P & H* _____

2. **SET OF TWO TAPES**
   NOW IS THE OPPORTUNITY FOR
   LIMITLESS PHYSICAL PERFECTION
   PART I – PART II
   $18.00 + $2.00 P & H* _____

3. **THE GIFT TO RECLAIM YOUR PROSPERITY**
   $9.00 + $2.00 P & H _____

*POSTAGE & HANDLING
Add $4.50 for Canada & Mexico
Add $8.00 for all other countries

BOOKS & TAPES SUBTOTAL _____
+ POSTAGE & HANDLING _____
TOTAL _____

(continued on other side)

NAME _____

ADDRESS _____

CITY _____ STATE _____ ZIP _____

COUNTRY _____ TELEPHONE _____

Please send check or money order for entire order to:
The New Age Study of Humanity's Purpose, Inc.
P.O. Box 41883, Tucson, Arizona 85717   U.S.A.
FAX # (602) 323-8252

WHEN PAYING BY VISA OR MASTERCARD, PLEASE FILL OUT AND RETURN THIS COUPON.

VISA ☐   MASTERCARD ☐

Amount to be charged _____

Account Number _____

Card Expires _____

PRINT Name on Card _____

Signature _____